An Afternoon
in Waterloo Park

An Afternoon in Waterloo Park

A NARRATIVE POEM

Gerald Dumas

HOUGHTON MIFFLIN COMPANY BOSTON 1972

First Printing W

ISBN: 0-395-13519-2
Library of Congress Catalog Card Number: 77-166471
Printed in the United States of America

An Afternoon in Waterloo Park

1.

I am sitting now at the dining room table
In the house where I was a boy.
Here last night my mother died,
Upstairs, at two in the morning
On that old thin rug on the
Bathroom floor. My father heard her fall.
He scrambled from his bed
And went to her and held her head
Until she died.
Or so he hopes.

She was old enough — born in 1891 — and tired enough
And often enough she had said she didn't care.
"Tired, tired, tired," she used to cry on the phone.
We would say to take her pills
But she had lost interest in medicine
And everything else.
"I'm old. It's time," she said wearily, weeping.
I could hear my father's voice: "Now, now."

And I wondered, is it possible to get so tired
You long to leave everything? Love and everything?
I wondered if it was in her mind, like Hemingway's,
That, sick to death of dull pain, dulled mind, futility, sick of
All things receding and retreating, even memories,
She preferred the grave to age's emptiness
And hoped to be remembered as she had been
In a sunnier time.

2.

This morning I was asleep in my bedroom
Across the country

And it was five o'clock when the red phone rang;
My brother said my name, and then: "Mom's dead."
I said: "Oh Carl," envisioned her face,
But could not hear her voice. One part of me
Hung on to my brother's solemn tone; of a million words
Between us, none meant anything at all
Till these. He had been an actor, and there was a proper
   pause
Between my name and the paralyzing news.

On the plane to Detroit I finally captured her voice
By pretending I didn't care, then turning suddenly
To pin it tight. I heard her speak her last words to me
Two weeks before: "Good-bye," then again, softer, "Good-bye."
Said sweetly, weakly, perhaps a little vaguely, as though
She were looking out a window, thinking of something else.

In the seat beside me a fat woman scowled sullenly at the sky.
I wanted to ask her, or someone: "Can you remember voices?
Always? Or just sometimes? I'm having trouble."
When I walked in the aisle eyes met mine and I
Wondered if they
Could tell. "My mother died. Has anyone else's?
Let's see a show of hands."

As a boy I would imagine an airplane full of ancestors:
I would sit in row A, with my father. Across the aisle
Sat my grandfather with his father, and so on,
Back to the plane's tail.
Except for me, everyone was about as old as he got to be,
Dressed in whatever he wore most days.
Then I would start up the aisle, slowly, studying faces
While they all sat there, gnarled hands on knees,
Smiling benignly, with one or two who didn't get to be so old
Eyeing me narrowly, disappointed in the way
The line had petered out.

None dying until he had begotten the next.
This was during the time I worried less
About those who died early
And more about those who missed the plane completely.

Beautiful glowing Sister Theo at St. Philip's had said
That we are made in His image
So I thought God worried about it too.

And I wondered if God
Wondered how He was going to keep us
Busy and happy up there. I knew that my own small demands
Presented no problem. God would ask: "What would you like
To do today? The airplane again?" I knew
He would manage it
Somehow. I only worried about my ancestors — would they be
Interested in this? They would have their own concerns and
I could see them itching to get away, grumbling
At having to sit there like that. There would be problems.
I would go up that aisle stunned at our good fortune,

Thank God God would be in charge.
Later there would be a planeful of my mother's people
To get lined up. Poor God. How many other quixotic
    projects
Would He be busy with? I began to see
That the best times might be at the end of each heavenly day
When we would lie around and tell
About the daily revels.

        3.

It is night. Everyone is gone
Except for my father and me.
I can see him through the dining room doorway.
With vacant eyes and trembling hands he sags on the couch
And stares at the fireplace grate, all stuffed

With gray ashes and crumpled scrap.
The casket has been selected and we have been to the florist.
My sister was particular about the flowers —
"She loved chrysanthemums, oh, and yellow roses."
But those weren't her flowers. If they could have been had
In October, and if it would have helped anything,
I would have surrounded her with marigolds, sprigs of spirea,
And lilacs. Hollyhocks, too.

4.

It grows late and my father continues to sit and stare.
I don't know what he sees.
But I know what he is thinking.
He is thinking about last night and he wonders:
Was she still alive when they took her out?
Why didn't I get into the police car too?
How was it decided that I was to follow in mine?
Why did I let the policemen take her?
At the hospital they wrote: DEAD ON ARRIVAL —
And my father wants to know if after forty-three years
Together she died alone in the back seat of a strange car,
While he was performing as mundane a task as locking the
    house.
He wants not to think that she opened her eyes
And looked for him, but saw only the black tangled elm
    branches
And dark second floors going by,
And heard only the lowering siren, now and again,
And knew she had only seconds,
Seconds out of all those years,
Seconds to look about,
Look in someone's eyes,
Say good-bye
Somehow.

It is a terrible thing to want to say good-bye
And no one to say it to.

In the backyard's dark he tried to unlock the garage door.
His fingers fumbled and shook — and then he fainted.
He struck his head on one of the drive's cement ribbons
And he lay there.
When he woke he knew it was a bad way for forty-three years
To end. And now he wants someone to tell him this:
She was already gone before the police came.
But no one can.

5.

The patrol car went up Dickerson between the sleepers,
Its siren warning drivers at intersections;
It warned the sleepers too, some of them;
Turning uneasily, they thought:
Something's happened to somebody. Not to me, though.
Not to me. Not now.
Not tonight.
Thank God.

They put her on a table in the emergency room, my brother
    said,
And examined her
And marked her dead.
An orderly and a jaded nurse came and looked at her face.
It was old, her face, and her hair was thin;
Her robe was faded and worn, like her body,
And she looked neither important nor beautiful.
Once she had been both.
They should have seen her as I see her
Here on the white dining room tablecloth, here in snapshots,
Some of them faded to colors of milk and caramel;

5

Some are pasted
To stiff black album pages, some are loose. Some are older
   than she was.
In these packed rippling pages is all her reality now,
All she knew of living — the men, women, clothes, cars,
Children, flowers, porches and brooms and cups and kittens,
Yards, towns, coffee cake and cushions —
They should have seen her as she was here — look —
She sits demurely on World War I grass, golden, soft,
Young in starched white nurse's apron,
Hair billowing shiningly out
From under the jaunty cap. She lightly holds a rose
And gazes somberly at it.

In the emergency room they brought a valuables envelope:
      FORM 160-A
      CONTENTS (TO BE LISTED)
      CURRENCY, COIN, TOTAL $_____
      OTHER VALUABLES:
And then, under NOTES, someone's handwriting:
      2 rings
      1 plain band
      1 diamond

They had trouble getting them off.

6.

My mother's name was Ingeborg Christina Friedariecka Holm
And they called her Frieda.
My parents were known as Floyd and Frieda; never
Frieda and Floyd. I used to wonder why. Now I think
Perhaps it is because the first trips better from the tongue,
While the second makes you stop
To separate the a's.

When I was told of all my mother's many names
I thought them lovely
And preferable by far to lifeless Frieda.
But here she is in Philadelphia
Training to be a nurse; she lounges on the roof
Of Lankenau Hospital, here in 1919, waiting
For the parade and General Joffre to pass. She laughs gaily
With nine others like herself, all with great blue capes
Slung carelessly over white uniforms
And strong white-stockinged legs; they gaze easily
Up the avenue
And lightly, fondly, sweetly at the future.

Below the fading moment, in white ink, are written all their
    names,
And once again I see that in those bouncy, bantering days
They called her Freddie.

To her mother and father she ever was
And always would be Friedchen; I used to hear
My grandmother, whom we called Oma, say it often
In those weak and loving tones that gentled
And subdued the German tongue.

To say that Oma and Opa, all through the 1930s when
They moved high and slow above me, were other-worldly,
Benign, venerable, would be true, I think;
To say that they looked like storybook grandparents
Would not be nearly banal enough; one should also mention
The way they lived and where they lived, in that place of
Great peace, that house of old brick, that kitchen
Of sunlight and foreign fragrances, that village of strange-
Sounding people whose German-coated English was a curious
Song encircling my head the whole day long.

I would have wished Opa a warmer man,
But no one who knew
Eugenia Herrman Holm, neither child, grandchild, neighbor
Nor acquaintance could find a flaw. Her finely creased face,
Her cheek, the softest and most mystifying I ever kissed,
Her slow, soothing, cracked-mellow voïce all invested me
With a deep wonder and deeper calm.
The house reflected her. Serenity, people said, such serenity
In that house. She was the gentlest woman I ever knew,
And those who had known her fifty years or more, they said
    so too.

Oma was sixty-three when I was born — I was twenty-five
    when she died.
That seems a reasonably long time to know
Someone from another land, another age;
But I wonder if it is, really. Two weeks
Each summer is all I saw of her and Opa,
Those visits and a few they made to Detroit . . .
And what is two times twenty-five?
A year, more or less, is that all I knew
Of her and she of me?
A generation of bright moments are what I have to show.
We sometimes touch those close to us
More briefly than we know.

I have one remaining note
She wrote to me in 1943;
Here it is, without a dot of change,
In its entirety:

      Conestogo, Jan. 1, 1943
        My dear Gerald.
      We had a fine day, the first day in
      the New Year. The snow is white
      and the sun is shining. The trees

8

looked like glass. I wish, you could
stay here. There is plenty snow and
ice, Ronny Forler tried his snow
shoes this afternoon. We don't see
many cars and the buss is not
running regular, because the Snowdrifts
are high and the roads are blocked.
Well as long the Baker and the Milkman
is coming, we are all right. Mrs. Holle
is coming with the water every day.
I am glad, you will all be together
tonight at Uncle Stan's, I will be there
too, you will find me in the big chair
near the Christmas tree. I am glad
you all had such nice presents and I am
sure mother looks fine in her new
housecoat and slippers. So my dear Gerald,
I must say good-bye, will write
a few lines to Carl.
God bless you and keep you.
                    Lovingly, your
                         Oma

"We're going to Oma's and Opa's tomorrow."
I stared at my sister. "Tomorrow?"
"Yes, tomorrow morning, Mama just said."
Evening packing: short pants, polo shirts, tennis shoes,
Extra belt, good shoes, Sunday pants, a tie, fielder's
Glove, hardball, good shirt, underwear, socks, and toothbrush.
Fitful sleep, then dressed and standing outside on
The six A.M. sidewalk, gazing at warm, hazy,
Strange Lenox Avenue. We ate breakfast standing, then bags
Were carried down the back porch steps.
Thirty years later, Svetlana Alliluyeva would write:
"Each of us has a sunny corner of the soul . . ."

In the heart of the peaceful German farm country
In Ontario, 196 miles from Detroit, there is a
Village called Conestogo. It has today and has always had
A population of about 400, and the people who live there
Now have the same last names as the names on the stones
In the churchyard cemetery.
At one end of the village wheat and corn fields
Curve away to the horizon; at the other the land drops off
Abruptly to a lush valley where cows graze
By a winding stream.

Once known as Musselman's Mills, it had been settled
In 1807 by Captain Thomas Smith. Then Mennonites from
Conestoga Creek in Pennsylvania arrived in their distinctive
Wagons and by 1853 the settlement had four hotels, three
Blacksmiths, a foundry, wagon shop, and several mills.
Huehn's general store went up in 1850 and stands there yet,
Unimproved, possibly unimprovable, settling in the summer
Sun, front porch bowing to the road, Herb and Oscar Huehn
Inside dispensing pitchforks and gum, sausage and straw hats,
Smoothing the yard goods, lining up the tubs and boots
And buckets. Snider's flour mill handled sixty barrels a day
And the brickyard began turning out the beautiful red bricks
That give the houses in that part of Canada a warmer touch.

The first session of the Municipal Council of the Township
Of Woolwich in the County of Waterloo was held in January,
    1850,
During which Redolphus Bargin was appointed assessor of the
East side of the Grand River, Conestoga; it was further agreed
Upon that a fine of five to twenty shillings would be levied for
Riding or driving faster than a walk over any bridge
Exceeding thirty feet in length.
By the fourth session in July of that year, Redolphus was
In trouble: "The Council having examined the Assessment roll
Made out by R. Bargin, Assessor for the East side of the

Grand River, and having found it very incorrect,
And other reports that have been made against him,
This council are of the opinion that another should be
Appointed in his place, and that he receive nothing
For what he has done. Carried."

And life went on in Canestoga Village, the spelling
Of its name changing from year to year, depending on
Who was reeve; they cleared trees and planted trees,
And they made some notes: "Maple, elm, basswood, pine,
Some hemlock and ash, cedar along the creek, and birch."
Around their homes they planted the now towering black
Spruce, and in 1892 they built St. Matthew's Church.
The talk was of sheaves and grain, the Heavenly Master
And weather, horses and chaff and hogs. Farmers died,
Sons took reins, trying to do it just the same,
Nothing changing much in village or field, and little
Note taken of the slowly moving age, decade passing into
Decade; a horse brought the doctor who delivered
Jacob Dahmer, and a horse took Jacob Dahmer to his grave.

While Conestogo was becoming modestly renowned
As a "village of fine homes, fine gardens, lawns and trees,"
Opa, newly out of Schleswig-Holstein, newly ordained a
Lutheran minister, drew closer to his old-age haven;
He and Oma were married May 1, 1890, in Williamsville,
New York; the following year my mother was born.
Johanna came, then Reimer, and in 1896 they went to
    Canada —
To a place called North Easthope. He was the pastor
Of St. James there for sixteen years. He wrote sermons
In his study, planted gardens, read, smoked, sped three
Fast horses about the countryside, painted watercolors,
Carved tabletops, bought a camera, played the fiddle,
Baptized, married, and buried.

In 1912 his horse threw and dragged him
And broke his hip. He was in bed for a year.
He became a sedentary treasurer of the Lutheran Synod of
    Canada,
And moved Jenny and the children to nearby Wellesley.
In 1918 they moved to Waterloo, and he taught in the
    college.
In 1922 he went to St. Jacobs, and then, a last two-mile
    jump —
To my soul's sunny corner.

Conestogo is not on the way to anywhere in particular
And even today few cars pass through. But in the 1930s,
With no television, few radios, and only thin strips of
Roads to connect it to the outer world, it seemed as remote
To me as any fairy-tale hamlet. The village and its curious
Inhabitants were different from anything we knew in the city.
Like Germelshausen or Brigadoon it might have appeared full-
Grown and placidly humming out of a
Suddenly parted summer
Mist, and even we children sensed that for a short time
We would live the lives of children of the past.

Opa's house had no running water, no refrigerator,
No heat save that from the
Kitchen's black and silver stove.
What it did have were old clocks, fine china, meerschaum
Pipes, flickering lights, flannel sheets, water pails
With tin cups hanging above, grape vines, an old barn,
Currant bushes, a strawberry patch, vegetable garden,
Tall grass to hide in, short grass to play on, single
Trees and rows of trees, two wells, roses on the walls,
A black iron fence with a creaking gate, and three
Tall spruce trees across the front that swayed and sighed
And lightly brushed the bedroom screens in the night.

It was all as old and worn and quiet
As Opa himself.

His name was Carl Christian Adolph Eberhard Holm,
Born on the island of Rügen in 1860, died eighty-five years
    later in Conestogo,
In the music room next to his study. He had a long white
Beard, a black eye patch, a five-inch heel on his right shoe,
And a collection of canes. On Sundays he used his glass eye
And his gold-headed cane and in his black clothes went
About his gardens as slowly as a king.
He both frightened and fascinated children and although he
Had taught Greek he seldom spoke English and never spoke
    to me.
He drank hot sweet Postum, put sugar on sliced tomatoes, and
Always cut his bread lengthwise into three strips.
He never came downstairs till ten.

Opa and Oma's marriage took place
Less than a month after their
First meeting. Under the glass on his desk was a poem;
All I could make out in it was the German word for "love."
I would bend over it each summer, trying to decipher the
Spidery German script with its passionate exclamation marks,
Trying to connect its ardor with the kindly but distant
Old man whose beard we children kissed each evening
At nine o'clock.

The bells were rung three times a day —
Six in the morning, noon, and six in the evening.
The villagers seemed to live their lives by the bells;
From the little louvered window high in the steeple
I could see them go in their houses each day at noon.
I used to wait for Mrs. Holle in the schoolyard and we would
Walk to the church and climb the twisting steps; I would look
    on as she

Stared at her watch, dropped it in her apron pocket, and
Set off the lovely clangor above.

Mrs. Holle was compact and powerful, her face homely but
Shining with wide humor and jaunty alertness. The only
Times I ever saw her serious were those moments when she
Took the thick ropes in her brown fists and with two
Impressive pulls set the bells going so thrillingly close
And yet so thrillingly high above the highest branches
Of the tallest trees. She pulled the bell ropes on and on,
Giving her whole body to it, her eyes intent on the floor,
Her thoughts far away, or simply counting, I never knew.
I wanted those Conestogo bells to go for hours; I knew that
The men in the fields heard them, the women in their kitchens
And gardens heard them, girls on porches and boys down at
The river heard them, every creature with ears to hear in
Every direction was listening to our bells, Mrs. Holle's
And mine, and I thought that I was at the center of creation.

At last she would wrap herself around one rope and ride it up,
Whooping and laughing, and the bells
Would stop with two muted
Clangs, and I would hear the buzzing and breezy-leafed world
Return, and we would go down the steps, I first,
Smelling the old dry rafters, cool walls, and the hymnbooks.

In the cool dawn, however, I was content
To lie in the snug bed
And listen to the bells, and after they were over, the roosters,
Far ones first and then the near, and someone pumping water,
And a Model A turning off the concrete highway onto a
Gravel side road.

We washed in our rooms out of pitchers and basins, sat in
A sun-filled kitchen corner, our Keds wet from the grass,

Eating bread and brown sugar and bran flakes, jiggling in
Our chairs, enjoying each mouthful and each moment,
Watching the highway through the window,
Seeing the milkman's horse suddenly appear and stop between
The trunks of two trees. We eyed Oma as she
Paid Mr. Martin out of a tin box and then we counted
Our own large Canadian pennies and planned our purchases
Down at Huehn's or across the road at Oscar Stroh's.
The blacksmith shop was a two-minute
Run and there was always
A buggy or wagon in front, for even the farmers who weren't
Mennonites used horses.
The blacksmith's name was Mr. Geise;
He had pale arms and all I ever heard him say was, "Ho, boy.
Easy, now." The farmers wore neckties, spoke softly, and
Smoked pipes when they worked in the fields.

Marty and Charley Schweitzer were our special friends;
They were in their sixties,
And they were good-humored, narrow-
Shouldered, big-handed men, stern with their huge horses.
They called pigs "picks" and potatoes "pitaytas."
Bachelors, they lived with their spinster sisters, Marian
And Sophie, in the same tall brick house where they had
Been children together.
The two-hundred acres they farmed lay
On all sides of the village, but their house, barn, orchards,
Chickens and flower garden were in
The village center, across from
The blacksmith and post office and only a moment from
The Trail's End Hotel, which their father had owned.

Charley's specialties were eggs and vegetables and driving
Them in his Model A to Saturday market in Kitchener; Marty
Was in charge of the horses, cows, pigs, and grain crops.

My brother and I worked in the fields with them and rode
Home high atop the hay wagon, waving to our parents
As we passed the house.

We played in old barns, ate homemade coffee cake in more
Than one kitchen, messed about the river for hours under the
Billowing sky, helped bring the village cows up from the
Meadows at five o'clock, and in the cool sweatered evenings
    watched the Conestogo Pirates
Beat all the softball teams for miles around because of
Russell Stroh's dazzling speed on the mound.

Late at night in bed, I would hear the faint clack of hooves
On the highway and I would kneel at the window and wait.
Then the swift beat was louder, a light filled the trees,
And down through the branches I could see the proud slender
Horse, a figure in black hunched over the reins, spinning
Wheels, a swaying lantern — then quickly gone, the sound
Dying slowly, so slowly, until finally all I could hear
Was the breeze stirring the leaves and spruce boughs as before,
And the clock far below striking the hour.

That was Conestogo in the 1930s and early '40s and there was
    also this:
Elderly Eberhard Holm resting
In his study; three houses down,
Reverend Wittig, pastor of St. Matthew's and a former student
Of Opa's, working in his; Mr. Kienzle, the mayor and
Postmaster, who had close-cropped white hair and the
Biggest head I had ever seen, drowsing away the
Afternoons behind the dusty numbered boxes, surrounded
By a hundred ticking pocket watches hanging on the walls;
George Dahmer, tilting on a wooden chair on the
Back porch of the Woolwich Town Hall, who would
Die at ninety without, it was said, ever once

Having left the village. We knew a handful of city
Things but he knew a thousand country things, and when
He or one of the other old ones asked with a kind of
Eager innocence a question about Detroit, I felt ill at
Ease and loathe to speak.
Cows were not herded down the street there,
Ancient men with long white beards were not to be seen
There, no anvils rang there, no bells were heard there,
Beds were not soft nor the grass as high there, green
Streams did not flow there, the sun did not shine clearly
Nor the rain fall cleanly there; so I mumbled and ran.
No point in thinking about such a place at all.

I don't know what Conestogo was to them,
But it was everything to me;
Little visitors sometimes notice
Conspicuous blessings that even whitebeards
In their wisdom cannot see.

7.

Is anyone in Hell yet?
Does anyone know?
How long do you stay in the cemetery?
Do you wear shoes and socks?
Could Raymond and me be in the same box?
I don't want to go.

Bedtime. We knelt at her knees
As she sat on our bed.
Her clasped hands and ours on her aproned lap.
There was a scent of sudsy skin,
A clean kitchen smell
As we chanted, "Our Father Who Art In Heaven . . ."

I was nine when I heard the news
That to miss Mass on Sunday was a mortal sin,

Sufficient to bar me from Heaven, entirely and forever.
From the moment I heard it
I didn't believe it.
In fact, I was outraged.
"What?" I mumbled, coming home from catechism, scuffling
    leaves,
"Do they mean that if I was fine and holy
Until I was ninety,
And then one Sunday said:
'I think I'll stay home today
And ride my bike,' and then — if I died right after —
God would peek through a crack in the gate
And say: 'Oh! You almost made it! You came *this* close!'
And gently shut it?"
No, that made no sense. And it wasn't fair.
Life is unfair, everyone said, but is God?
Judgment Day isn't. Is it?
I had to admit, though, that I was quite disturbed
By the Good Thief on the cross.
Here I was, a saint till ninety,
With only one late tragic slip —
And there he was, evil all his days
Until his final hour,
When through sheer *luck* he happened to be
At the right place at the right time!
Now who deserved Heaven more? Him or me?

Nine years old, and discarding dogma.
I envied my small sister her restful plea:
"Mama, am I good enough to go to Heaven
So far?"

        8.

He has gone upstairs to bed now,
To bed in the old house he began to buy

In 1940. Three rooms up, three down,
Winding, creaky stairs between.
A bleak and blemished house but I didn't know it then,
In 1940 when I was ten.
He paid six thousand for it — slowly, very slowly —
And it was twenty years before he said: "It's ours."
He was making thirty-eight dollars a week then,
Walking twelve miles a night at Parke Davis & Co.,
Checking doors, watching, listening, wearing a uniform,
Carrying a gun. He had been a bus driver,
Salesman, creamery worker, clerk; and for a time
In the thirties he'd been out of work. But now —
Thirty-eight dollars in a tan envelope on Fridays
And a house on Dickerson Avenue.
He was heartened at the upswing in his fortunes.

Dickerson looked better in those days;
Now elms, like old neighbors, have vanished. Dickerson
Is open, bare, hard-edged, every bump and scar visible,
Like a leg out of a stocking.
The houses are tall but the elms were taller,
Spreading out above the street to meet and mingle,
A leafy roof for our play.
Ours was the only house on our block without its tree —
Because, I guess, of the squat red hydrant I saw used once
In ten years, when the Brady's garage burned down —
And our small lawn at noon was a bright dot,
A hot green jewel in all that dappled shade.

The streetcars on smooth Charlevoix at the end of our block,
They are gone too and sitting here in the night
I miss their reliable, organized rumble.
Streets now are stuffed with cars, packed grill to trunk,
And fuming buses. Boys no longer practice grounders
In the street the way Ralph Smith and Artie Blount and I did,
Scurrying sideways, pouncing deftly,

All fine precision, concentrate! on a dirty white
Adhesive-taped ball, with only occasional quiet Packards,
Jaunty '40 Fords and boxy Dodges to stop us.

And so I lived on this street, in this house,
From the time I was ten to the time I was twenty,
When I went away.
Only ten years, but they loom larger in memory
Than all the happy others.
The Dickerson years, years dominated by my mother,
How they stalk my days and nights . . .
Years of chalkdust and newspaper bags,
Red cabbage and red-cheeked, rough-tongued quarterbacks,
Dogs and bikes, priests and fountain pens,
Playgrounds and peanut butter, tennis shoes and aunts,
Mass and ice men, Jack Benny and knickers,
Hank Greenberg, screen doors, Orphan Annie, lace curtains,
Classrooms, coal trucks, Mars bars, and knives.

Through this — at the center of our lives — moved my
     mother,
Short, strong, scrappy, sick with menopause,
Mostly unhappy, sometimes screaming,
Occasionally singing, filling me with terror
And fried eggs, wanting love, spreading gloom,
Confusing my days and rending the nights
With her anguish.

What I want to know now is:
Who was responsible for her troubles?
Did she perversely refuse to brighten things,
Preferring endlessly to grumble and lament her lack of love?
"I have nothing," she would cry, weeping on the kitchen table,
"I have nobody. Nobody." I didn't understand.
I wanted her to be as happy as Mrs. Wasek. I wanted to have

Everyone love her. But I could only stare impassively
As, shaking and helpless above her, I reached out
Hesitantly to pat her heaving back and hot damp neck.
Had she always been like this? Was she born like this?
I need to know how much one person can blame another
For being the way he is.

And is it unfair, my memory of my mother?
She did laugh, she did sing and smile,
She did sigh, giggle, delight in her garden,
And look fondly at me now and then.
But often when I think of her I see her
Wailing, arms out and rigid, while I, ten, cry
And run to close windows. My sister wrings her hands,
Her face bunched in grief; my father runs into the room
From somewhere.
"Change of life," I heard them say, but I knew
She was no ordinary mother. How many other mothers
On our block ever lay in bed, moaning,
Forearm over eyes for two weeks? Home from school
For lunch: "How are you, Mom?" and no answer
Though I knew somehow she heard.
"Are you getting better, Mom?"
And I would go down and make myself a sandwich.
They took her to a long gray hospital on Jefferson;
She had electric shock treatments and in time returned,
Walking slowly up the driveway, commenting
On the peonies, asters, and the others
While my small heart rejoiced.
She dwelled too much on herself,
She was easily displeased, wanted her way, was affronted daily
By persons known and unknown, and had
No trouble seeing the
Shadows of a sunny day; yet —
I could see in small moments she wanted desperately to lead

Another life . . . serene, gracious, wise — who would not? —
Could sense it, see it, just beyond her, always just beyond.

And so I sit here tonight at her dining room table, looking
At snapshots of her life, dumbly wondering,
And wondering too
What she'd say to me if she knew. "What's all this?"
I think she'd say, and laugh a short embarrassed laugh.
I run my fingers along the heavy old tablecloth where it
Drops over the indented edge. I remember the feel of it
From long ago, know it better than today's toothbrush and
    telephone;
Strange to think a dead person placed it here.
The house is filled with small last acts. I stood in her room
Earlier, looked in her closet, stared blankly at the dull
Cotton dresses, gaped at the few pairs of shoes,
Handled the paltry pins, the necklaces, replaced them
In her neat, bare drawer.
I am as filled with loss as my life once
Was filled with her.
I seem to be weeping for her.
And for me.
And for all of us.

9.

I remember
Lying in bed at the age of twelve
Listening to St. Philip's unfeeling chimes
While the smell of frying bacon envelops me;
A thin clatter of plates in the kitchen,
The shallow clink of a cup,
And my mother singing softly to herself.
My sister stirs next door, opening drawers,
Parting hangers to find a dress.

A sudden water spurt across the hall
Cleans lather from my father's razor,
Then all is still. He is dressed except for uniform
Shirt and tie; his right arm biceps bulges whitely
Above his tan forearm and hairy muscled hand.
I hear Carl's voice below, a clinking of his car keys;
The side door opens and shuts; he clears his throat in the
    seven A.M. air.
He walks across the street. My window shade flaps.
His Hudson starts and he steers it, straining, from
The curb, joining the scuttling cars that advancing
And receding have an urgency
They never have at night.

I stretch, and scratch my side. A good day starting.
My mother's singing voice.

10.

Before we lived here on Dickerson
We lived two blocks over, on Lenox,
In a two-family flat.
It was all two-family flats on Lenox,
Drexel too, and Springle and the others;
These streets were packed and populated with
Young children, old children, aunts, uncles,
Seminary students on leave, soon-to-be nuns, invalids,
A sprinkling of grandparents, great-grandparents,
A girl named Edith with rickets, a wide and strange
Assortment of shapes, nationalities, and degrees of happiness.
The men were factory workers, clerks, teachers, grocers,
Firemen, policemen, mailmen, and men out of work.
All tall men, to me, when I was between three and nine,
And all wearing hats; I sat on my front steps and saw them
Walk home from work, trudging heavily, seriously, and with a

Curious dignity.
Once in every ten houses or so there lived a laughing father
With energy to spare and youth enough to put his lunch box
Down and sprint away in grinning circles
From squealing, chasing children on the small front lawns
And crumbling sidewalks and around the maple trees.

Their wives, endless trickles of them, padded up to corner
    stores,
Stern as bankers, housewives in white anklets, cheap hats,
And thin print housedresses, and I could never tell one from
    the other;
They were unlike their own children, each child wondrously
    unique,
Like a box of books; and my mother moved
Among these women
Transparently, sweeping the porch, pinching dead twigs.

Those old sketched lanes I saw and loved on someone's
    wallpaper —
Where were they really? Did they exist, those curving,
    dipping,
Picket-fenced roads, cottages set at random angles
To each other in a tangle of hedge and fence?
In New England, someone said, and Virginia, and a hundred
    years ago.
Then who decided we had to live on these rigid grids?
I knew that beyond the city were the careless clusters
Of village yards and farms and fields I loved,
But here someone in authority had said, "Closer together, those
    houses,
Closer, closer, that's it, and make them more the same."
And now they were.

My mother, see her here at twenty?
She wears a velvet dress that brushes her high-button boots;

She is curled into a hand-carved and
Cushioned chair, on the lawn
Of her country home. A fragile cup sits in its saucer nearby
And she reads poems beneath the boughs of a spruce tree.
She was spirited, pretty, clear-eyed at twenty
But strangely not married until thirty-two;
Soon she was living on Lenox, walking to the corner stores
And you couldn't tell her from the others.

Here and there among Detroit's interminable
Two-family flats and maple-planted streets
Were other streets, unaccountably elm-lined,
One family under each sumptuous roof —
As though the planner had shrugged: "Oh, I suppose
We could spare one or two; let them have their extra bit of
    room."
Lakewood was one street, Dickerson another,
And everyone wanted to move onto them,
To get happier.
The ones who did move, maybe they were happier —
Maybe some of them stayed happy for a very long time.

II.

When I was four
I used large parts of spring and summer days
For playing cars on patted roads in clay
Between tough grassy tufts, plantain,
Soldiers peeping from root embankments, keeping
Watch over porch-step fort.

When I tired I picked dandelions, held
Their stems too tightly, smelled them,
Not liking the smell, only the bright yellow
And softness and tickle
On my small nose tip.

When I tired of that
I watched caterpillars and butterflies,
Not knowing one would become the other,
Not knowing I would become a soldier,
Speed down wide clay roads.

Does a butterfly remember
How once it slowly toiled?
Or know how ugly sluggish then
And how pleasing now?
Does it realize that's how most people see them?
Would it agree?

12.

Sun through a window
Falling on my young forearm
Lighting blond hairs.
Outside the morning-glories
On our wire fence
Wave their blue and white bugles
Gently to me.
The top of my head and my arm feel warm;
I want to be out on my tricycle
But am not allowed just now, I don't know why.
I have been good, the day is nice,
I am not sick or sleepy.
My mother paints the back porch with gray paint;
I go to the kitchen door and ask: "Do you get stuck
When you stand on paint?"
She doesn't want to talk
Or let me out to ride my trike.

At four o'clock on summer afternoons in the city
Small boys on my block were called inside
To get cleaned up.

We were bathed and dressed in white cotton blouses
With large buttons on which our short pressed pants were
    hung.
We reappeared, blinking, into a different sun
To lightly play and talk till supper.
We didn't know that we were poor.

On a cold September morning
I was awakened and brought trembling
Into the warm kitchen
Where my mother on her knees dressed me
For my first day of school.
I spilled my oatmeal
And said nothing that I can remember.
She put a sweater on me
And I followed my brother through the gloomy living room
To the front door. The morning sun was hard and glinty
And I walked behind my brother and Chucky Moore
From next door, my brother's black-haired friend.
Up Lenox to Kercheval, along Kercheval to Coplin,
Up Coplin to Carstens School — immense brick building! —
And to kindergarten.

We lined up; a tall kind lady with a face like a hawk
Took our names. There was Frank Fetters, whose hair,
Yellow and straight, was to turn mysteriously dark and curly
Overnight, at thirteen; Allen Smeltzer, who one spring day
In fourth grade, by the swings on the south playground,
Would show me the spot where his sixth finger had once
    been;
Fat, genial Marjorie Dearth, who lulled me into dreamy states
With gently drawn pictures on my back as we sat cross-legged
On the gym floor listening to *Babar the Elephant,* read softly
By a grim lady in green bloomers and bowling shoes;
Laughing, placid, big Art Wasek,
Whose beautiful broken-Englished

Latvian mother served us sweet rolls, hot chocolate,
And bowls of canned peaches on
Dark winter afternoons; husky Robert
Hulber, whose lyric tenor voice,
Lately found, stirs audiences now in Salzburg, Stuttgart,
Milan and Rome; sweet and serious Isabel Wren, who would
     die at nine
From drinking poisoned ice water, intended, by her
Silent raging brother, for their father;
Alan Burley and Ed Valeko,
Each of them dignified, unruffled, capable, responsible,
Elderly at five and ever after;
And all the fine young athletes, Keith Bennett, Jack Doptis,
Johnny Allen and Dick Wolff,
Leaping, loud, joyous, and always
In mind's eye with sweaters on,
Shirts out beneath, and moving,
Moving, moving; Chuck Schneider, friendly,
Shaggy, furtive, who
In fifth grade would invite Earl McGinniss one garage's length
Into an alley where they bent
Their heads close over a small, worn
Photograph, courteously declining later to show it to me;
Buck-toothed Tom Jefferson, moccasined
James Monroe, close friends
Into high school, whose sorely tried teachers took satisfaction
In telling them year after year to
"Live up to your name," which
They might have, it seemed to us later, without that heavy
     burden;
Tall, saintly Shirley Krist, fat-calfed Katherine Mulere,
Mary Ann Franzoni, who loved me, and Jeanette Minaudo,
     whom I loved
And who in sixth grade, informed of
My yearning by George Curtis,

Would write a nine-page letter to me, about me, about us,
And on the way to school one morning would tell me she had
Something for me, and at the corner of Vernor and Coplin
Would take it from her bag, hand it to me, gaze at me with
Solemn brown eyes, snatch it back, tear it into dime-sized bits,
And drop it forever unseen down a storm drain.

Carstens School occupied an entire block; it had south
And north playgrounds at its sides, trees and lawn in front;
I was to grow to know each crack and gully of its abused,
Undernourished earth, watch buds of those trees unfold into
Leaves hour by dreamy hour over eight slowly rolling springs.
On frosty mornings big girls with flying curls skipped rope
While hard-running packs of boys swooped and screamed
In wheeling crescents; older boys gathered seriously
In cindery alcoves to flip war cards with their bloody scenes
Of the Chinese-Japanese slaughter; others in corduroy knickers
And high-top boots stood about chewing Clark bars, lengths of
Black licorice, Necco wafers, and Milky Ways.

But on that first day it was noisy, shrill, terrifying —
Until we were let in and calmly introduced to paste, fish glue,
New crayons, piles of fresh paper, boys' lavatory, shears,
Distant, sleepy-looking George Washington, wise, petulant
    Lincoln,
Jovial President Roosevelt, Simon Says,
And all the singular smells of school.
Everything was either big or little —
Little Gym, big Gym, little Art, big Art,
Little kids, big kids; big and little teachers too.
The big ones were frightening — they walked heavily,
Knowingly, plodding about with alarming rings
Of jangling keys.

Slowly it all grew warm, inviting, familiar; we endured
And were passed from one teacher to another:

Miss Ireland, third grade, lordly and loud, reprimanded
Me for making old-fashioned capital G's, which I preferred
And had copied from my mother ("Stand up. Is this the way
You were shown? Is it? Who wrote this? Answer me.");
Miss Mahoney, Social Studies, tiny, witty, wore glasses
That looked like bottoms of Coke bottles, taught us eraser tag
And played it superbly with us up and down the aisles;
Miss Cane, Auditorium, who seemed to suffer inside herself,
Endlessly, stiffly implored, "Please form a straight lion";
Mrs. Diebold, fifth grade, of pince-nez and sardonic smile,
Mystified us when her easy wit in halls would spark placid
Mrs. Sullivan and glum Mrs. Parker to twinkling life;
While beautiful young Miss Adams, regal, gentle, prematurely
Gray, distributed Oh Henrys each Wednesday for best themes,
Let us choose books during free time, showed flickering films
Of Model T trucks racing along empty concrete highways
To forest fires, listened to us carefully,
And looked at us closely.

Old red-haired moon-faced Miss Maher, the principal,
Heard me sobbing one morning and found me sick and
    shivering,
Crouched inside the mauve swing doors of the cold, damp
And puddly basement lavatory; I was in sorry condition,
And rejoiced weakly at the sight of her.
She washed me and calmed me and drove me home
In her blue two-seater coupe; sitting beside her I felt small,
Important and guilty, for suddenly I felt infinitely better.
My mother opened our front door and I drifted dolefully in,
Trying to look worse than I was.

Later, when I was nine, I lied and called:
"I'm going out to play!" but instead
Walked all the way to Jefferson and Alter Road,
To a funeral home,
To see Miss Maher in her coffin.

13.

I see myself at age four
Squinting in the sun, wearing a summer
Sailor suit; my young arms are pale, impeccably
Soft and bland; I know how those arms are to touch,
What they smell like.
I would like to enter the snapshot, step
Through, lift that little boy off his bike,
Play with him, see what he's like, see if
I like him.
And I wonder if he
Would like me.

14.

The life of a boy is filled with furtive action —
Stealthiness, guilty grab and slinking,
A sudden start at the sound of a footstep —
These are what he knows as well as anything.
When I was with Raymond Leslie, the catalyst was
His mother's large and gleaming glass jar of dark brown
    sugar.
Mrs. Leslie was a twinkle-eyed, laughing, generous woman
Who made taffy with Karo syrup, let us do the pulling,
And sent prettily packed boxes home with me.

I was never sure that it was necessary to steal the sugar,
But Raymond seemed to think so; in time I knew
It was the only way he could get some excitement in a house
Where all good things were free.
So I would crouch with him in their pantry, popping
Tenderly lifted lumps into my juicy mouth, listening gravely
To his mother's washday banter in the yard below,

And the clothesline's squeaky, signaling wheel.
The uses to which innocence is put!

With Harold Weinger it was his father's big white heavy
    handkerchiefs,
Which covered the lower half of our outlaw
Faces as we skulked
Behind garages and around alley corners; but nothing
In our games of guns could
Equal the excitement of standing in
Harold's father's forbidden bedroom,
Examining the rich contents
Of his dresser drawer; there were usually a dozen or more
Handkerchiefs, neatly stacked and lightly scented; Harold
Would say, "Shh! I'll fold them up and sneak them back in
    later,"
And then he'd take a dime or quarter or whatever he was in
    the mood for.

Harold's mother never liked me much.
She liked me even less after one September afternoon
When with a murderous yell I leaped off their front porch,
Through some junipers, and onto her back, thinking she was
    Harold.
She howled and dropped her groceries, but she was stout
And I was small and anyway I only grazed her. I sprawled
At her feet, jumped up, and for a moment we were face-to-
Handkerchiefed-face. She scowled at me, then
Eyed the scattered contents of her broken bag.
I thought she was looking for something to throw,
So I ran into the Brooks' backyard
And crawled beneath a tangle
Of stems and branches. I took deep cold breaths,
Wiped my nose with the tip of my and Mr. Weinger's
    mask —
And noticed for the first time the large and lovely

Embroidered "W" near the bottom, just above my sheriff's
  badge,
Just above my black and hammering heart.

Later there were other friends and other broken rules;
Our wants exceeded our supplies and we got away with
What we could.
The endless rules, the endless line of crafty, grasping boys!
All so normal — until the time when little thieves
Will feel no guilt.

15.

Does God laugh?
Boys wonder.
Upon being introduced to God
We wanted serious replies
To questions like these.
But they told us, "God is All Just,
God is All Powerful, God is All Knowing,
God is All Wise."
Outside we asked each other,
Could you tell God a joke? Or was He divinely sad,
Always knowing the punch line?
Had He ever once said: "That's a good one! Boy,
What a funny ending."
We felt bad about it. With all the misery
God knew about, He couldn't
Laugh at a joke.
They hadn't said anything about His being
All Happy.

It sounds as though we were a saintly bunch,
Thoughts winging piously heavenward, eyes wide and holy
As we stood around on the playground, innocently snapping
  gum,

Gouging stones from the clay with the scuffed tips of our
  school shoes.
Well, we weren't.

We ranged wide, pondering next
On our own excrement (an unknown word then),
Wondering how long we could dine on a portion
Before all the goodness would be gone out of it.
God, Eternity, Nutrition —
Our curiosity kept easy pace with our ignorance.

My mind is filled with absurd notions,
One crowding after another . . .
Just now at midnight I thought:
Last night my mother undressed and went to bed
For the last time ever.
She hung a dress on a hanger for the last time,
Said a prayer, drank water, felt a towel, looked at a clock,
Smelled the night air, turned on her side for the last time
  ever.
Once again she is dead to the world for the first time
Since the moment before she began to live.

I see in mind's eye an epitaph
For a gravestone — not hers — mine, perhaps.
The bottom line reads:

Well. That Didn't Take Very Long.

16.

My mother, like anyone who lived lengthily,
Had several lives, maybe four or five;
I really only knew her during two.

I look at the snapshots — a moment comes
When I don't see how they could all be her:

A child
In sun-filled straw hat, careless spilling
Pale hair, quiet eyes, budding nose, a sip of a mouth,
White dress and stockings, polished black high-button shoes,
Seated on the back seat of a buggy
Behind her fiercely bearded father
And a huge and shining horse named Rex;

A slender young woman, resplendent nurse,
Leaning gracefully, lightly, against a country garden gate,
Ready for love and life,
Ready for anything;

A Detroit Depression wife, formidable mother of three,
Taut, red-knuckled, solemnly vigorous, thriftily
Hoarding pennies, planting tiger lilies and peonies
In worn-out clay;

A middle-aged woman in a middle-aged century,
Legs thinning, skin spotting, waist and neck thickening,
Ever-aproned at sink and basement ironing board,
Cutting grass sometimes, sweeping snow, lining shelves
With yellow paper, watering plants,
Reading the *Free Press* on the porch,
Beginning to think she'd been doing it forever;

An old woman, sick of the city, sick of strangers,
Sick of noise and fumes, sick of her clothes, of neighbors,
Of making dinner, sick of the way she looked,
Sick of being sick;

Sometimes it seems to me

The one I loved most
Was the one or two I never knew.

17.

I look at this picture of that old man,
My grandfather,
And my eye drops past the full-blooming beard
To his hand, pale, strong, as hairless as the
Top of his head; a hand used to pens and desks,
Used to pipes, pump handles, hoes, a horse's flank;
A hand knowing of heavy Bible, wafer pages,
Golden edge and gothic script; an 1860 hand
That knew the 1860 things. And it startles me
To think that my shy hand once lay in his,
As his lay in his grandfather's, who flourished
While Napoleon, to name one, still lived.
From me to 1800 —
And one pale hand the link.
A touching chain, and longer than we think.

18.

The Monteith Public Library rises like a friendly fortress
At the corner of bungalowed Eastlawn and commercial
    Kercheval;
It towers above bakery, drugstore, hardware, and bar.
With its turrets, tall narrow windows, and massive stone
    blocks,
It looked to us as though it had been a castle, a lonely haven
Around which puny civilization had crept until now,
Like an old ship gone aground, it was being put to other uses.
It was eight blocks from our house but I knew it well,
Knew its high iron fence,
Worn cement steps, oak doors, and porcelain drinking
    fountain,
Dormant in winter, in front.

The Monteith Public Library was a summertime place —
Visits were rare in snow — and boys sped there on bikes,
Baseball gloves hanging from handlebars.
Girls walked. They always walked. They seemed to have
    more time.
They sauntered slowly in summer dresses, cradling thick novels
Between tanned, sinuous arm and scant waist.

As though ringing a doorbell I felt compelled to taste
The cold river water at the freely flowing fountain
Before going in to the deliberate calm, coolness,
And intimidating order that seemed worlds away
From the moiling street outside.
The musty history, the humor, the accumulated tales
And science of centuries waited for me on the high brown
    shelves,
All man's delvings and wise jottings bound down
Into bicycle basket size.

I wandered about plucking books, sniffing the new pages,
Inhaling the smell of heavy curtains, smooth waxed tables,
And lofty, dusty peace,
Smelling all the lovely intelligent smells
Of the Monteith Public Library.

19.

On a sun-filled Monday afternoon in May
My catechism class and I silently descended the stone gray
    steps
That led from our cozy chalkdust classrooms to the quiet
Dappled coolness of the church. We slid into pews at the rear
Between two confessionals
With their dreaded thick red curtains.

We were eight years old and about to make

Our first confession.
Banks of votive candles flickered red and low in front;
Saint Joseph and the Virgin Mary, in painted plaster,
Stared impassively down at empty pews; she held
The Infant Jesus, fatter than any baby I'd ever seen;
The grown Christ stood nearby, dark, lean, pointing
With two languid fingers to His exposed and sacred heart;
Here again He had no smile, not the hint of a twinkle
    anywhere.
He had rather the sad, speculating look of a man waiting
In a dentist's office. Without knowing that I knew,
I began to understand why; for with
Anxious heart, locked fingers,
And frenzied head, hunching sideways
Ever closer to the curtain,
I suddenly saw that there was nothing funny about
The intricate business of getting to Heaven.

Time grew short. I went over the Ten Commandments once
    more,
Uselessly, for I was quite aware that my problems lay
In numbers five and eight.
Thou shalt not kill, I'd read, and *Thou shalt not bear
False witness against thy neighbor.*
Nothing simpler if you are eight. I had wondered that people
Could be bothered by these or any of the others.
But then our attention had been directed to finer points,
Which someone had taken the trouble to append to each;
And gathered under number five I saw: *Do not be angry
Or unkind to others. Do not wish them harm.
Do not hate them. Do not fight or try to get even.
Did I? How many times?*
Several thousand times would have to be my answer.
Apparently no provision made, either, for who started it —
Just getting involved was enough.

And under number eight:
Do not make a bad confession by hiding a big sin.
Do not say mean things of others.
Do not tell lies.
There was no way out of it — I would have to tell about
Breaking the Weingers' window. With a piece of rope.
Who would have believed a piece of rope could break a
    window?
When Mrs. Weinger had shown up at
Our door, black hair wild
And flashing-eyed, to say that her Harold had said I did it,
I denied it.
Actually it had only cracked, not broken.
Despite that distinction, I knew I had lied, boldly, in cold
    blood,
And for the very first time.
I had felt particularly bad about it because,
Although Mrs. Weinger had not believed me — my mother
    had.

There was only one ahead of me now, Edgar Senick, and in he
    went.
I bowed my head and read: "O my Jesus, I am sorry
I have been bad, because I have displeased You, Who —"
My eyes opened in terror — I could hear Edgar!
I could hear Edgar in there, telling his sins!
"Yelling at me, so I hit —" I heard him say.
Carelessly I cupped my hands about my ears, slouching low,
Giving no sign, I hoped, to Betty Inesen, next to me.
Dear God, I didn't want to hear Edgar! I might have listened
To Betty, though. I guessed it would be a fairly bad sin,
Although I hadn't seen it covered anywhere.
Suddenly Edgar's rough hand appeared, and then his rosy face.
He smiled sheepishly and went away to say his penance.
And then I was in.

I waited tensely while Father Killian heard the other side.
Then the screen slid back, the dim outline of his face leaned
    close,
And he said, "All right, go ahead."
I said, "Bless me, Father, for I have sinned. I have done
The following sins —"
And suddenly, crushingly, to the surprise of us both,
I began to cry.
I sobbed, heaved, whined, sniveled, and choked out
The story of the Weingers' window. Father Killian, stunned
At my wordy torrent, hushed me finally and became,
To my surprise, reassuring, sympathetic,
Hopeful for the future, and all that anyone could ask.
Pulling myself together, using my sweater sleeves on my
    cheeks,
I said an intense Act of Contrition;
Father Killian absolved me
In comforting Latin of all my sins and told me to go in peace.
Feeling holiness steal through me like coffee up into a sugar
    cube,
I checked my eyes, nose, and mouth, straightened my sweater,
Tucked in my shirt and went out.
Betty Inesen eyed me sharply.
"You cried," she said smugly.
"I did not!" I hissed, wheeling sharply for the front.

I took eight steps, maybe ten —
And stopped. It was incredible.
One second out of the confessional,
And a liar again!

   20.

Children giggling, fathers joking,
Puppies wiggling, kittens rolling,

Brothers tickling, neighbors grinning,
Milkmen whistling, girls clapping,
Nuns twinkling, Ralph Smith cackling,
Eyes crinkling, laugh lines growing,
Lips spittling, classes howling! . . .

While, looking down from altar heights,
Museum, school, and kitchen walls,
Gazing out of ribboned missals, calendars
And somber frames,
Was the ruminating, melancholy,
Distant, odd and ominous,
Phantasmagoric, following, and
Grieving eye of God.

21.

It is a black and bitter winter evening in 1924.
My father is crossing Gratiot near Racine, sees too late
A car come at him fast; he leaps, seeing just before the leap
A woman's face frozen over the wheel —
He rolled over and over in the mud and snow; some men
Ran out of a drugstore, carried him inside, found that his leg
  had been nearly
Snapped off; white bone showed below the knee, and his foot
Dangled heavily by shreds of tendon and skin.
He heard them say that the car had not stopped.
They took him down to Receiving Hospital
Where a doctor said
The leg would have to come off.
He insisted that they leave it on, then slipped into a dream
Of snow in black and bones in red.
Later in a ward he woke and for the first time saw Frieda
  Holm.
He saw the crisp apron, the cap, the scissors;

She smiled and tended him.
She and Jo had both come to Receiving; it was closer to
   home,
They had been invited by an old surgeon who valued their
   skills,
And they had both been ready for something new.

The leg was infected and was long in mending. Months later,
On crutches, he shyly posed, his black hair thick and straight,
On a Belle Isle rock with the young-looking Canadian nurse.
Jo had met Stan Wilson by then; Stan was a large brash self-
Assured city patrolman stationed in emergency; he had a car
And the four of them went everywhere together.

Stan and Jo were married in the summer, in Canada, by Opa.
She wore a bridal gown and veil and afterward they all
Posed in the garden.
The next snapshot shows my mother and father in February,
   1925;
They have just been married and they stand on a Gratiot
   sidewalk
Outside the Catholic rectory; you can see their prints
Behind them on the lightly snow-dusted rectory steps.
My mother wears an embroidered coat and a large hat.
My father carries a new tan overcoat and a cane.
He is done with being a city fireman; she is finished
With her nursing career; together, after returning from
A honeymoon at her parents' house, they will move into
An upper-floor flat on Drexel and he will look for a good
   job.
My father will limp the rest of his life, painfully
Some days — and my mother will remember the bare quick
Circumstances of her form-signing wedding morning.

A meeting of fender and flesh and all was changed.
An unknown woman drove home, read the papers next day

To see if she had killed. She hadn't — but for her
And for endless others to come,
The pattern, the maze, was again rearranged.

22.

Here I am, my back to the camera, bamboo pole and line
Over my shoulder as I look at the meandering Grand River.
My father must have snapped the picture there in 1938,
But mostly I was down along the river all alone, or
Under the bridge that stands there still, or
Upriver at the crumbling concrete dam
Where I would lie on a smooth flat rock with my
Brown hand sunk in the cold smooth current, or skimming the
White froth. I smell everything,
The yellow slippery underside of stones, a barbed-wire
Fence, the cloth of my pants, the rubber of my shoes,
And when I hear the rooster halfway up the hill at
Dahmers' farm I can smell the chickens, their dry feathers
And their feed and the floor of their house and the
Dust of their yard.

I wait on the bridge as a
Horse and buggy come down the hill.
I like the sound of the big thin wheels on the stones and
The hollow rumble as they come onto the bridge.
The Mennonite farmer and his children stare as steadily
At me as I do at them. I have already learned that
They will not wave or smile or speak. There is only a
Mild curiosity on their faces, which for a moment pierces
Some airy barrier between us. I watch them clop and sway
Away and curve up the hill to their farm at the top.
The children look back at me. I think of
Them as my friends.

43

I am home for lunch, seated at the dining room table
Beside Opa, with Oma across from me.
My mother is speaking German, and laughing and passing
And cutting. The house is filled with the aroma of
Snyder's country sausage, my spoon is engraved *Mai 1, 1890,*
And the well water is fresh and cold. I am surrounded
By sights and sounds and smells I adore.
I have lived a long and heady life the breezy morning long,
And this afternoon, I know, there will be more.

23.

In bed.
In my old boyhood bed.
Drifting and waking and turning and sleeping
And dreaming of my mother dead.

From this room I used to leave for catechism class
On Monday afternoons, where I sat and wondered
How God could keep from getting bored
In a paradise filled with perfect souls.
I thought that if God is like men, even a little,
He'd want to look in on Hell occasionally.
Who could stay interested in endless streams
Of holy sycophants? Or maybe the saved won't be
Like that. Perhaps out of necessity man is changed
Into a more Godlike creature who knows the proper
Thing to do or say, at any time on any day.

If I were God, I might long ago have invented
Equal Gods, to have someone to horse around with.

Sometimes I think that God could have done a little
Better than this planet and the fettered lives,
The often terrified and tiny lives the unlucky poor

And ravaged and sickly and crushed have lived on it.
If we know that then He knows that.
So He probably did.

24.

It is morning. My father and I fumble about in the kitchen.
I open drawers, cupboards,
See bowls, bent tablespoons, a spatula,
Meat grinder, dented saucepan, some of the first objects
I ever saw and touched. Thrift, luckily for us, was in her
    blood.
I go out into the backyard with a cup of coffee to get
A sniff of October air, to scuff the leaves.
And just look around.
It isn't Saturday but it seems as though it is; I see men
Working in nearby yards, in and out of garages,
Men who work
Weekends at the plant.
When you hear or read
Something like, "The country . . . the land . . .
The United States of America," what images come to mind?
Whatever you are most used to, I suppose.
I see a day like this, the hardworking innocence of
A Saturday morning in fall, with men in red plaid shirts
Carrying stepladders and rags; their wives inside windows
Pointing to missed spots; leaves riding on burlap, being stuffed
Into baskets and boxes; paper boys, pockets sagging, collecting
Silver at front doors; dripping cars and unruly green hoses
In driveways; mothers thoughtfully
Unpacking groceries, laying in
Cartons of carved-jewel Cokes,
Crouching at the refrigerator door
In an aromatic cloud of cold salami, shifting things around;
Teen-age boys moving silently about the house,

Trying to forget
That they are soon due on an emerald field in full football
     gear;
Older people nestled in sunlit corners like sleeping cats,
Brooding over editorials, scrutinizing bills; boys calling
To each other, straddling bikes, announcing plans;
Aunts stopping by to deliver a platter, a skirt, a drop of
     gossip;
Uncles leaving to get boats out of the water or clean up
Odds and ends at the office; humanity moving in and out of
Hardwares, gas stations, dry cleaners, bakeries . . .
I always felt a special modulated joy, a deep and
Quiet happiness that was Saturday's own,
In this land and in this time.

25.

Breakfast.
My father sits in his armchair at the head of the table,
His back to the windows and the plants on the sills.
His hand shakes. Coffee spills into the saucer.
He puts the cup down and looks at his hand.
He says softly, "Isn't that something?"
I shake my head in sympathy, remembering.
While getting the silverware out I found our old napkin rings.
My mother's and father's are silver, mine is a green plastic bird
With a black bill. He stood by my plate,
His bill over the edge, waiting for me; he heard everything.
Sunday dinners were at two.
We had a roast with browned potatoes
Or a stewing chicken with mashed potatoes.
I see Sunday dinners
Always in summer, a fan blowing air from the living room,
The ball game turned down low, with sometimes a rush from
     the room
To see if the roar was for Greenberg or York.

Then we read the *News*
And the *Times* on the porch while someone
Went to Commenator's for
A quart of vanilla. We wore white
Shirts and the street was quiet.
I remember weekday dinners in autumn;
It is dark outside, warm
In the kitchen; there is a smell
Of leaf smoke and apples at the door; a
Hamburger-onion-tomato-pepper-macaroni
Casserole is on the table,
And I am wearing slipper socks. At one or another dinner I
    heard of the deaths
Of Carole Lombard, President Roosevelt, Mr. Vanadia two
    doors down;
I heard of the start and the end of
World War II, of my father's
Promotion to Fire Marshal, and one evening my brother
    shout:
"I fail to see why the children should
Be punished for the passions
Of the parents!" My sister looked confused, my mother
    gasped,
Carl ran upstairs.

But now a quarter of a century later my father and I
Sit alone. The sun shines on his back.
We stir our coffee. Conversation is difficult.
He doesn't want to talk of either the past or of the future.

The doorbell rings.
"Who can that be?" he says mildly, which is what my mother
Always said. She was constantly astonished at the ringing
Of the bell, as though someone were trying to climb in the
    window.
I open the front door and see a Negro boy of seven or eight.

He holds a brown, wrinkled paper bag. He squeezes it tightly.
He says nothing. We look at each other solemnly.
"Hello. Who are you?"
"Charles," he says.
"Where do you live?"
" 'Cross the street."
He indicates the house the Reynoldses used to own.
I never saw much of the
Reynoldses; no one did. The only thing
I remember about them is an incident that happened
In 1945, one hot summer evening about six o'clock —
There was a sound of crashing glass and a prolonged scream;
My mother said: "Did you hear that?" and we all ran outside.
At first everything looked all right. Then we saw
That one of the Reynoldses' second-floor windows
Was broken. Glass fragments lay in the bushes and on
Their lawn. Suddenly there was another scream and a
Crash of glass in the next bedroom, and we saw a bloody arm
And fist sticking out. It belonged to their older son,
Lately returned from the war. We had seen him briefly,
Sitting on the front porch, tanned, black-haired, handsome,
Glowering. He never spoke.
The neighbors were gathered now and we saw Mr. Reynolds
Behind the broken window grappling with his son, and we
Heard more screaming.
A police car came and they took the son away.
I never saw him again.

"How are you, Charles? Would you like to come in?"
He looks past me for a moment and shakes his head no.
Black families have moved into about half the houses
On the block now, and several of the remaining white families
Have For Sale signs on their lawns.
My father has never been anti-black;
I remember him speaking

Fondly of Negroes he had known and worked with all over
   the city,
And he knew a great many. But recently on the phone
He had spoken of "the stream of black" going by.
He would be working on the lawn, he said,
And black boys and girls
Would walk by and laugh at him,
And he didn't know why they
Were laughing. They would see him picking up bits of paper
   and twigs,
And they would drop candy wrappers and cigarette butts
And they would spit gum out,
And then they would laugh at him.
He said the parents seemed to be all right. He agreed
That white children litter too. But he began to talk
About the stream of black going by.

Charles studies me for a long time. He is good-looking,
Slight, short-haired, and is wearing new sneakers.
Suddenly he hands me the bag. "My mama says she sorry
To hear about what happened. She says to give you this."
Charles watches me closely as I take the bag.
"Thanks, Charles. This is very kind of you."
Charles nods and goes down the steps.
I shut the door, sit down on the piano bench,
And open the bag.
Inside there is a large jar of instant coffee
And a small can of condensed milk.

26.

Mrs. Middleton called me across the street this morning.
She was sweeping her front porch steps with weak, stabbing
Strokes and looked up and saw me staring at her.
She is somewhere in her eighties and looks like a

Retired charlady. She has lived on Dickerson longer than
Anyone else, lived there with her aging bachelor son Ralph,
Who in the forties worked the night shift at Dodge.
Ralph took very good care of a gleaming 1940 Ford,
Which he kept in the garage and seldom drove. Ralph's eyes
Always looked feverish and he smiled a lot and never said
    anything.
When we first moved in I asked him something or said
    something
And he didn't answer; he simply grinned for a long time.
I felt uneasy and didn't speak again. He seemed content
    enough,
Never as far as I know looking our way for the next ten years
As he smiled and smiled
And fixed his glittering eyes on the can of wax and soft cloths
And the unmarked finish of his unused Ford.

My mother had liked Mrs. Middleton. She could detect faults
In other neighbors but she never said anything against Mrs.
    Middleton.
Perhaps it was the simple directness, the earnest lack of guile
That my mother also had and that
Was typical of the farm women
She had known in her youth that allowed them such
    rapport . . .
I used to see them
Talking animatedly on the sidewalk, aproned
And broomed; you could see that they got along.

Mrs. Middleton wore old slippers around the house, and put on
A black coat and black straw hat when she went out.
Her legs were heavy, her face ruddy, and her white hair
Partly unpinned; wisps and strands drifted along her cheek
And in front of her eyes.
The only time I took an interest in the Middleton house

Was the moment each summer when her daughter and
   grandchildren
Came to visit from St. Louis. I always went quiet and forgot
To breathe whenever I saw the green car with the
Missouri plates
In the driveway, for one of the grandchildren was a girl
With long blond hair and the loveliest legs I had ever seen.
Summer after summer she came from
St. Louis to sit for a week
On the front porch swing, wearing white shorts, her legs
Crossed, or tucked, or flung; she read books, her fingers
Dreamily sliding through locks of hair, riding slowly out to
   the tips.
When I left our house, or came home, or stood on our porch,
I would look at her and she would glance at me,
But we never spoke.

"Come inside," Mrs. Middleton said. "I want to give you
   something."
She labored up the steps and we went in.
"Do you like cups?" she said.
She took her broom to the kitchen and came back
To the front hall.
"Sit down, sit down. I've a set of cups you might like."
The shades were drawn and there was only one light on.
The air was stale and the rooms were crammed with furniture.
"How's Ralph?" I said.
She opened a closet door and drew out a package. "He's all
   right."
She gazed quizzically at the package, fingering the strings.
"Now what's this?" she said. She stood for a long time
   holding it
And staring at the floor. Then she said, "Oh yes," and put
It on the sofa with two others.
She went back to the closet and took out a stool. I asked if I

Could help but she did not reply. There were several boxes
On the shelf; she selected one and stepped down.
"I think this is it," she said, and blew dust off the top and
Rubbed off the rest with the side of her hand.
She brought the box slowly over to me and opened it.
"I buy things and save them. I get them on sale. Nice things.
I wait for an occasion and then I'm always ready. These are
Nice cups. I gave a set to my granddaughter."
It was a set of six coffee cups with riding and hunting scenes
And snow scenes and one of Christmas.
I thanked her and said, "Your granddaughter from St. Louis?"
She went back across the room. "Yes. Married a dentist.
Got a boy and a girl now." She carefully placed the stool
Back in the closet and shut the door.
"They visit me every year
Or so. She asks about you sometimes. Always wants to know
What happened to you."
We walked to the front door. She was breathing heavily as we
Got there and she folded her hands at
Her waist and peered out
At the street. "Your mother kept me posted on your doings."

As I went across to our house I looked back and waved.
She nodded her head and beamed behind the storm door
And kept watching me through the narrowing crack as she
Slowly swung the main door shut.
It was the first time I had been inside her house.

27.

Mount Olivet Cemetery is at Six Mile and Conner,
Just past the old city airport if you are coming
From the direction of our house or the river.
We just came back from buying a couple of plots there,
My father and I. Today it wasn't like in t   old days.

In the thirties, when summer Sunday afternoons
Were long even for grownups,
When there was no television, little money, when
Most people kept their church clothes on all day and
Did not believe in doing any sort of work, what
Was there to do?
If you had a car you could go for a drive.
You could go for a drive, and visit relatives.
If you wanted to be sure the day remained peaceful,
You could visit dead relatives.
You could go to the cemetery with flowers and a sprinkling
Can, stand around a while under the weeping willows
And listen to the birds and the quiet.
On the way back you could pull off Conner and park
At the chain link fence, drink icy Cokes, and watch the
   DC–3s
Take off and land just a few breezy feet away.

I used to think of the airport and the cemetery
As being a pair, part of one another,
Like salt and pepper. And now I see
That they were linked more than just geographically;
In each there is the same unyielding emphasis
On arrival and departure, an awareness of time
And its duration, the sensations of space, destination,
And the pervasive thrill of impending doom.

My father's mother, Louisa, had been buried in
Mount Olivet; a large, laughing, earthy Ma Joad of a woman,
Who vowed smilingly that she wouldn't let the cancer get her
   until Floyd's
Second boy was born, she drew her final breath
Two weeks before my tardy arrival.
She had seventeen children, but only
Ed, Helen, Emma, Philomene,

Harold, Floyd, and Francis survived her.
Eleven years later her husband
Joseph died at eighty-one. He had been
A shipbuilder and lumberjack, following his gnarled trade
From Wilmington to New London,
Bay City to Detroit, building
His own house wherever he went.
He was a tall, tough old man who would come over on
  birthdays
To smoke an ancient pipe, grin silently, and press quarters
In our hands. At his funeral my cousin Gloria stood
On the red velvet kneeler and reached over and touched his
  hand.
"He's all cold!" she cried, and someone hissed, "Get that child
Away from there."

Uncle Ed remained outside. They said,
"Come in, Ed. Aren't you coming in?"
I looked up and saw him shake his head.
"Ed never looks at anyone dead he knew," Aunt May
  whispered.

I watched my father all that day, I remember, looking
For some sign of grief, relieved to see him impassive;
But that night at the table he put his fork down
And covered his face and wept: "I used to take his lunch pail
To him when I was five. He used to stop and laugh when
He saw me coming. He used to pat me on the head."
It was the first time we had seen our father cry.
We sat stunned, our heads bowed, tears creeping down our
  cheeks.
My mother got up and went around to him and cradled his
  head
Against her apron.
He apologized brokenly for spoiling our supper.

My mother held him and said, "Now, now, honey."
I think this was the first time for her too.

All those years of going to
Mount Olivet, and I had never seen
The main entrance on the far side, nor the offices.
We went over sites with a sandy-haired man named Felden
And picked two plots in section Q.
It was in the new section, he said, and would look much better
In a year or two. We drove over and looked at it.
My father stared at the earth, his face as frozen as on
His father's funeral day.

What do you think about when you look for the first time
On the place where your body will lie for all eternity,
Or at least until the merging is complete?
Nothing, probably. Probably nothing at all.
We got back in the car and started out of section Q.
Beyond the fence across the street, a woman hushed a crying
    baby
And carried a bag of groceries into a house.

28.

Three weeks before my ninth birthday, on May 14th, 1939,
I advanced haltingly to the altar rail at St. Philip Neri Church,
And with a hundred-odd boys and girls and a finely racing
Heartbeat received my First Holy Communion.
The white cloth had been flipped over the length of the rail
By two altar boys, brothers named Eagan,
High school football stars. I knelt
And slipped my scrubbed hands beneath the linen, scooped it
Under my chin, and slightly stunned, frantically trying to finish
My fifth Act of Contrition, stuck
My tongue out and felt for the

First time the Holy Body of Christ enter and stick to the roof
of my mouth.

Sister Theo had said to swallow the
Host instantly; neither then nor
Hundreds of times thereafter was I able to —
I always wanted to
Take a poll and see how it goes with others — so I let it
dissolve,
With occasional prods from my tongue, until it was
thoroughly in me,
And I was in a shining state of Grace.

On the way back to my pew,
Hands pressed mightily together in front of my throat,
Fingers tightly straight and skyward, I concentrated
Not on God, not on heaven, not on the post-Communion
prayer,
But on my expression.
Eyes were on me — I knew that. I was almost nine now,
Consecrated at last to Christ and Everlasting Goodness,
And it was my intention to look a lot different
From the snotty little sinner (as some forgotten backyard hag
Had christened me) of a moment ago.
The question was, how did one go about radiating holiness?
I knew that in time and with experience it would be no
problem,
But I felt an obligation to show proof immediately of
My newly exalted state; I had even gone so far as to
Hope that God would provide each of us with an eerie,
enveloping glow,
Like a candle in fog, an outward sign
Of our suddenly purified souls.
It seemed to me that the thing to do was to
Look as much like a priest

As possible — pious, serious, grim even,
Yet with just a touch of incredulity at the awesome meaning
    of it all.
I had watched the first ones coming back; the girls were
    better at it.
Perhaps a bit too prim, too humbly noble, eyes shut too
    fiercely tight
(How could they see?), but still preferable to the boys,
Many of whom had gone forward trembling, as if to get a
    shot,
And come back in obvious relief, grinning faintly, searching
The mottled throng behind the last row of white veils and
    shirts.

And so I tried to steer a course halfway between; unsmiling
But relaxed, head bowed yet triumphant — at peace again with
    God.
Crumpled back in the pew's haven I hid my face
And said the prayer we had been taught:
"My God and my All! I love You! I love You! I love You!
O my God, I believe in You!
O my God, I hope in You!
O my God, I love You with all my heart!
You have given Yourself to me, dear Jesus.
I give You myself. Take me and keep me close to You.

Keep me from sin.
Help me to obey.
Teach me to be good and pure and true."

The last part of the prayer was all right, I thought,
But the first part troubled me.
Those exclamation points indicated a passion
I couldn't muster. I said the words with what I hoped
Was a proper ecstacy, but I got the feeling

That I was trying to talk myself into something.
I envied that high plateau of love the author of those words
Lived on and was upset at my inability to get there too.
Yet I also loved God.
I loved my idea of Him at least, although I had to admit that
Usually when I thought of
Jesus or God the Father (They looked
Much the same except that the Father's hair was white
And He had put on some weight), I pictured myself
Loitering on the fringe of a large group,
While His sad clear eye swept casually about, resting on me
Momentarily, then passing on, like a football coach
Searching moodily for some small sign of talent.
I knew that I could never initiate
The least conversation with Him, let alone
Cry: "My God and my All!
I love You! I love You! I love You!"
He seemed too calm for all that.
I thought it would embarrass Him.

I glanced across the aisle at Jack Griffith
Who at Thursday's rehearsal had hoarsely whispered to Carl
  Bielow,
"You take him," nodding chillingly toward frail Peter Fallon,
And then, his hooded squinting eye on me, "And I'll take care
  of him."
Griffith was the toughest guy around,
With a face to match his fighter's instinct.
Already he looked battered, wise, experienced, his speech
Gruff and harsh as his scabby fists.
Bielow was a bully, no match for Jack, a swaggering, loud
And brutal braggart — I had no use for him but I respected
Griffith's competence, his badger courage, his Bogartian
  hardiness.
What whim compelled him to designate myself and Fallon

As two who required special care I never knew,
For I'd begun devising rules of conduct of my own,
Self-Preservation being very near the top; so outside
I didn't hang around to see what Griffith had in mind
But made thoughtfully for home.

And now, while Bielow gazed aggressively about,
As though he'd like to take the bloody church on,
Griffith dreamed listlessly, like an aging champ, it seemed to
    me,
Of missed and lost encounters, of dwindling powers,
Of empty hooks and jabs.

Bishop Mooney began to speak: "Grant and preserve in me
A pure and spotless heart; be Thou ever more dear to me
Than sinful pleasure, than all the good of this world,
That I may bear anything, suffer anything, lose everything,
Even life itself, rather than lose Thee,
And Thy grace."
We piped our smooth response: "Graciously hear
And bless me, O Jesus."
Bishop Mooney: "May Thy benediction rest on my parents,
Relatives, benefactors, friends and companions; to Thee
Are known their anxieties, needs, and wants."
Children: "O Jesus, bless them."
I reflected warmly on the welcome words, "My parents,"
For this meant the church embraced my mother too;
I hoped she'd heard it back there in the rear
And was not weeping —
For often lately I had lain in bed at night
And heard her almost incoherent cry: "The Catholic Church
Is taking my children away from me!" My father's
    reassurances
Were unavailing; her sobbing lasted hours,
Interspersed with sudden shouts, as they occurred to her;

Finally I would fall asleep, as drained and weak as she,
My brother's arm around me, as the waves of silence
    lengthened
In the living room.

She frightened me and hurt me and too much time
I trembled and wept with her as I lay in the dark and listened
To her litany of wrongs — and yet her grief was real
And I was sad to think she thought herself alone, this
Devout believer in her father's faith; for I never thought of us
As in two parts — she was my mother
And a member of Messiah
Lutheran Church — it was a fact of life, like living in Detroit.
Why make so much of that?
The truth I think was perhaps that
The devoutness of her own belief was nothing as compared to
Her devout nonbelief in Catholicism.
And so I cringed when Bishop Mooney said: "Do you believe
All the Holy Catholic Church teaches, and just as she teaches
    it?"
We all said we did, and gave the rock-built reason why, and
Bishop Mooney said again: "Then say with me: I give Thee
    thanks,
O God, because Thou hast called me to the true Faith,
To Thy holy and infallible Church. I profess,
Solemnly and publicly before Thee, Thy holy angels and elect,
And before this congregation, that I firmly believe,
And hold as truth whatever Thy infallible Church teaches.
With complete submission of my understanding, I will
    faithfully follow
The doctrines of this Church, and will never separate from it.
A Catholic I will live and die."

What was she thinking back there?
What was she thinking now?

I thought of the moment when I had walked into my room
And had seen my new Communion clothes laid out upon the
  bed:
White shirt, the sleeves extended wide, blue tie, blue knickers,
Blue knee-length socks and new black shoes — all arranged
  precisely so,
As if enclosing an invisible paper doll. It was the way she did
  things,
At least it was that day, and I wondered if she cried,
Gazing at the empty clothes,
As though I'd already gone away.

29.

Uncle Ed was the eldest of the seventeen children
That Joseph and Louisa had; my father was third
From the youngest, and since Ed ran away from home at
Sixteen, he and my father were relative strangers.

Ed hoboed around the country on freight trains for a time,
Worked at odd jobs from Seattle to New Orleans, then
Went to sea. He got his engineer's license
And steamed in and out the world's ports deep in
The greased and oily heart of ocean freighters.
Eventually he returned to Detroit and became an engineer
In the public schools. Rumors of illegitimate children
Trailing in his wake, he courted and after
Many years married Aunt May; became,
To my mother's later regret,
My godfather; and took to dropping in on us on
Sunday afternoons,
When he would tell stories, fight with
Aunt May, and never remove
His black knit seaman's cap and peacoat no matter
How long he stayed.

Uncle Ed and my mother never hit it off.
He represented everything
About my father's family she disliked. Ed was loud, crude,
Stubborn, undomesticated, assertive, sinful, and happy.
He was also my favorite uncle.
Ed was a big man, bigger even than Aunt Jo's
Husband, Uncle Stan, with long strong arms and hands,
A thick neck, short gray hair, no teeth, and only one eye.
I knew that Opa had lost his eye in a youthful chemistry
Experiment; I never knew where Uncle Ed lost his.

In 1936 when my father fought to
Get work and earned five hundred
Dollars the entire year,
Uncle Ed came over with three huge Easter
Baskets wrapped in purple cellophane;
He barged in the door one
Snowy Christmas eve with three sleds.
When he ate his supper —
He and Aunt May never seemed to eat
Together — it was likely to be twelve fried eggs on a platter.
He ate with a tablespoon, and the knit cap was still on his
    head.
They lived on Waltham, near the end of
A long block of look-alike
Houses all in a row. Ed had built his own house, and it was
    small,
Small and rough and peculiar; and he placed it at the rear of
    the lot.
On Sunday evenings he would hush guests
So that he could listen to
Charlie McCarthy. He would laugh so hard that no sound
    came out,
And his one eye would become a wrinkled slit,
Matching the look of the

One that was gone. He would get out the family Bible
    sometimes,
With all the dates and names in front,
And tell me how he had gone
Through church records in Montreal and
Quebec City, turning the
Brittle pages with a knife,
And found that the first Dumas in the
New World was a physician who had come
Over from Paris with Jacques
Cartier in 1535.
Uncle Ed told me that when he died he would leave
The Bible to me; he did die, but I don't know what happened
    to the Bible.

One drab Sunday afternoon he drove us to a lonely stretch of
    track
To show us how to hop a freight.
We watched through the window
While that tall and tough and fifty-year-old man loped
    alongside and
Swung up and rolled into a boxcar. He dropped off two
    blocks away
And walked back down the track grinning at us.

I went into the engine room at Carstens one school day and
Asked the old man there if he knew my Uncle Ed. He was
    leaning back
On two legs of a chair near the furnace door and he said,
"Do I know Ed Dumas?" He turned to the young engineer.
"Here's how Ed Dumas cooks his lunch."
Picking up a long poker,
He said, "Ed takes a Polish sausage, see, and he sticks it on
    here
And then —" He opened the furnace door and I saw the
    orange flames

And felt the heat. He shoved the poker in and swiftly drew
   it out.
"That's the way Ed Dumas cooks his lunch."

Uncle Ed drove our family to Conestogo the summer of 1934,
When we had no car.
I remember nothing of the trip, but here
Are the snapshots. "He didn't realize how far it was,"
My father once said, "and woofed the last fifty miles."
Aunt Philomene came along too and I don't know how we all
Got in the 1933 Chevy.
He was a kind man, and he had a raucous
Sense of humor. I used
To wish my mother liked him better than she did.
Even from her
Point of view he was not completely hopeless. Here in the
Snapshots he is wearing black shoes, white trousers, a white
Shirt and — for his first meeting with
Oma and Opa — a tie.

30.

Today I saw a lovely girl pause
At a drugstore window, then drift inside.
She had a lonely self-collected look, as though
Used to being by herself and liking it.
Her hair was long and brown, her body gently curved,
Her cheek and collarbones high and finely thrusting.
Our eyes met for an instant, then she was gone,
Then we were both gone.
She was one of those special girls, languid, with
Wise and quiet eyes; when you see such a girl
You fall a little in love, long to hear her voice
To see if she has it all, but you know she does,
They always do.

I saw one come sleepily smiling out of the Hôtel de Seine
On Rue de Seine one summer afternoon;
She was shining at the boy whose arm she held,
And I felt dry and outside life
As they softly swirled away.
I've seen them in Phoenix, Boston, London, and Oslo;
I saw one glowing once and she saw me beside Route 1
In Maryland, near the Conowingo Dam, and another one
In another year in church in Defiance, Ohio.

I saw two in one week in Quebec, and one out at Percé,
On the Gaspé Peninsula. They flower in unlikely places,
These girls of searching and somber glance, and I think
None knows how unique she is —
Or that there is a man somewhere remembering sometimes
How on a train he started when he saw her face
And crossed legs
And slender blue-veined hand
And amber beads and sandals and
That still he sees the book she held
And remembers that their eyes met a moment too long
That warm day, twelve, or two, or
Fourteen years ago.

31.

St. Philip's had four priests as a rule,
The pastor, Fr. Uhlenberg, and three others
Who would arrive, become popular, or disliked,
Or feared, and at the Archbishop's whim, we gathered,
Mysteriously depart, like a traded outfielder.

Fr. Uhlenberg stayed on and on, bald, stern,
Grimly pious. His were the only sermons that

Did not put me in a light coma; generally he
Was boiling about something, bawling out the entire
Congregation, grown men and all, fearlessly, an old
Fox terrier growling and snapping at sleepy livestock.
His surliness commanded my attention and respect.
The assistant priests could not seem to get the juice
Of everyday life into their sermons, which were filled
With abstractions, wispy, cloudy trails of gauzy theory,
So packed with words like "covenant" and "confraternity"
That my mind drifted up and out of the church along with
    the words,
Where we parted.

Their vocal praying disappointed too. On occasions
Such as family funerals my mother would hear the rosary said,
Swiftly, flatly, without feeling but rampant with rhythm.
In the car she would shake her head and
Berate the praying priests, and in the dark back seat
I would silently agree.

Typically, the rosary resounded: "HAIL Maryfullof grace,
The Lordiswiththee, BUL-LESSED artthouamongstwomenand
BUL-LESSED isthefruitofthywomb, Jee-zuz."
And we responded with resolute, rhythmic fervor, all but
Stamping our feet: "HOLY Mary, MOTHER of God, PRAY
    for us sinners,
NOW, andatthehourofourdeathamen."

In their defense, I supposed that anyone whose career
Called for them to say aloud thousands of Hail Marys
Would be forced sooner or later to adopt a pattern,
Certain emphases, basic, unvarying inflections — I knew
That if they were ballplayers they would swing
The same way at each letter-high pitch. And yet —
This was different.

66

I wondered how Mary herself felt. What suited her?
Slowly, with feeling, or rapidly with a nice beat?
And was it important to say so many? She seemed to me
The sort of lady to whom you would want to give
A single perfect rose.
My Uncle Will, Aunt Philomene's husband, was a tiny,
    waggish,
Rumpled runt of a man, and his wake was the first I was
    ever at.
It was there that doubt began that fifty Hail Marys
Or a thousand and fifty would have any effect on the
Destination of Uncle Will's departed soul. It seemed to me
That he ought to be required to stand on his record.
"Intercede, we beseech thee, Oh Queen of the Heavenly
    Hosts . . ."
Said the priest, and I saw her approaching the golden throne
And saying to God the Son
(God the Father I saw as being much
Too busy to bother with Uncle Will, at least right now, and
God the Holy Ghost I saw as a little too vaporish to be
    consulted),
"Look," she would say, "a lot of them
Down there would like you to
Do something for Will Mannes, and I think you should too."
That's what intercession meant to me, and I couldn't see it.
How could you nudge someone into Heaven?
What if he needed one
More nudge and never got it?
Would any amount of prayers save
Uncle Will if he had been beastly? Mary was no fool —
Likely she would
Reply, "No, I'm sorry, he was beastly." I couldn't see her
Troubling God about it, and I couldn't see Him vacillating,
    saying,
"Well, I don't know . . . maybe you're right." The one thing

I was certain of
Was that God wasn't wishy-washy.

Just as I was getting straight in my mind the way praying
Should sound, a Father Kerry arrived at St. Philip's and
Once again I was thrown into uncertainty, though not
At first. Father Kerry looked and sounded more like a saint
Than anyone I'd met up to then. His eyes when open burned
With a holy heat; when shut they shut so tightly,
So intensely, I thought someone must be jabbing him
In the spine with a letter opener. And when he prayed!
Never had I heard such feeling, such emotion,
Such bowed concentration, such passionate, low-keyed
    conviction —
One would have thought he was a Lutheran.

Father Kerry stayed on at St. Philip's several years,
And I never stopped thinking him gifted, compassionate,
And fervent. But one Sunday morning a thought came that
I was unable to shake: Was he concentrating so diligently
On sounding right that he could think of little else?
Can you think of two things at once? Perhaps all the priests
Who intoned so flatly found that dispensing thus easily with
Words, they were free to keep a holy bead on the meaning.

I felt lost again. It would be fine, I thought, if Christ
Would return, look about, and say, "No, no, no, this is the
Way I meant it." Many might pay Him no more attention
Than before, and others might never get physically close,
But somewhere, perhaps watching Him on
Paramount News, throngs of us would at last have learned
The proper way to say a prayer.

32.

From May 1, 1890, to May 1, 1940, that's a full fifty years,
So Opa and Oma came to Detroit on a silver Canadian train
To celebrate, toasting each other at Aunt Jo's Saturday night,
Sitting for the camera Sunday on kitchen chairs in Uncle Rim's
Backyard, just the two of them, his country minister's old right
Hand around her now plump shoulder, then all of us together
Gathered round them. He was eighty that year,
An elderly flowering tree, his beard spread over white vest
And black suit, his lines and planes a sculptor's joy.
Oma, serenely seventy-three,
Nibbled at lunch and smiled across
The yard at me, as I in knickers and new tie clasp darted
And hovered half-listening about the family fringes.
I was in the last month of being nine. I loved having
Everyone older, didn't want it ever to change. I wanted only
To stay close to these seasoned old ones, I the quiet runner
Running in their windless wake.

Late Sunday afternoon I sat high on the stairs over our packed
Living room while Opa spoke of student pranks in Kiel, of
    mustard
And a bedsheet; he laughed long and weakly, his eye wet and
    shining.
I had never seen him like that and it was the only time I ever
    would.
Aunts, cousins, uncles, they howled and shifted and joked,
My father beamed, shook his head, my mother —
My mother softly laughed and watched her father,
Her nervous hands a blur,
And up above, behind the rail,
I kept a springtime watch on her.

33.

Once, half an age ago, I heard my mother recall
How it was when death came to the North Easthope families
In, say, 1910, when her father
Would conduct the funeral and she
Would play the organ sitting all alone
In the loft. Any man in the church could have dug the grave;
Often two friends of the dead man, if he had any,
Volunteered. If the deceased were a child, the father
Might want to do it and they might let him.
There was plenty of room behind the church;
An iron fence and a row of spruce and hemlocks
Separated the dead from the rolling fields.
My mother said that she would stand beside Oma
And Jo and Rim, and she would hear her father slow
Down every time he said, "Ashes to ashes, dust to dust . . ."
It often was winter when the dying came, and the digging
Was hard and the snow would fall and she saw Opa bald
And bareheaded in the snow reading the old verses,
Reciting the old prayers, ignoring the wind
While his beard flew about.
And when it was over the old black-garbed farmers
Would nod briefly, shuffle in their hunched way
Out through the gate to their buggies, silently help
Their women up and go away.
It must have been quite simple and direct, then,
Disposing of the dead. A minimum of paper
And numbers. But look at this paper with its numbers
I've just pulled from my jacket pocket.
It is a sales slip, and says:

An interesting sum of numbers
For such a simple thing.

The price itself was reasonable, I thought,
Surprisingly so. Fifty-one square feet.
Enough room for two, and forever. Why,
Considering what you pay today
For land you only own until you die,
That's a bargain, wouldn't you say?

71

34.

She had a limited view, my mother did,
Of the proper things a woman should do.
As I grew up I wondered at and felt exasperated by
Her narrow rounds. Her interests were few,
Beyond housewifery: the morning news with Austin Grant;
Gardening; the Messiah Lutheran Church at Lakewood
And Kercheval; and gossip.
Whatever she did she did with a will;
When she was well no other mother on our block could
Match her industry. Nor, said one, did they feel the need to.

World War II, when it came along, drew her attention
With a vengeance. Germany, with its sprinkling of relations,
Was the magnet. If the enemy had been any other nation
Her interest might have been limited to ration booklets.
When some poor soul came over and damned the Nazis she
Would come to an instant boil — she made no distinction
Between one German and another — and many a softly
    buzzing
Sunday afternoon was ignited by the fury and fight of her,
The never quite concealed scrappiness that inflamed the
Normans and the Lillises and the others, none of them loath
To speak, either — before coffee and
Sunday supper took the edge
Off their various appetites and they parted, heartily enough,
She to her kitchen sink, the company to their cars, and the
Rest of us to the restoring cheer of Charlie McCarthy, Jack
    Benny, and Fred Allen.

Baseball, so much a part of Detroit's life, baffled her and so
She ignored it.
Barney McCosky, Charley Gehringer, Tommy Bridges,
Pinky Higgins, these names meant nothing
To her. She never saw

A major league game; she never saw me play anything but
   catch.

Hardball and softball teams divided and multiplied like cells;
From the ages of five to fifty, everyone seemed to play or
Watch; each diamond in the city was a world of its own on
Weekday summer evenings.
Strange wealthy teams would arrive
In complete uniforms from unknown neighborhoods; they
   would be grim,
Talented, hard to beat.
Ragtag teams with no uniforms would make
An appearance and they would be lightheartedly inept.
Most teams wore caps, any old
Pants, and two-color softball shirts
With advertising on the backs. My first shirt said: MOE'S
   BILLIARDS,
Paid for by an even-tempered and tiny
Hunchback who gave me dime
Tips and free Cokes when
I delivered *Colliers* and *The Saturday*
Evening Post and *The Detroit News*
To his pool hall. My second shirt,
Orange with black sleeves, was donated by
Jacob Schaeffer of the
Schaeffer Funeral Home;
He was to hang himself a few years later
In the basement.
A thoughtful, considerate man, they said he was
Found naked but for his glasses, and only a few feet from the
Embalming table.
My final shirt was from the prestigious DeSantis
Funeral Home, whose teams
Invariably were splendid. Mr. Jerome
DeSantis was dark, small, kind, popular, and regularly the
Most generous contributer to St. Philip Neri Church.

My mother washed that shirt endlessly in our basement's cool
Dark, ran it through the ringer, carried it outside to the bright
Backyard, pinned it to the line,
Noticing perhaps how the DeSantis
Letters slowly shriveled and the black sleeves went to gray.
You could not escape DeSantis at our house, for his calendar
Hung year after year by the basement stairs and his
Sobering half-page advertisement in the parish bulletin
Confronted us each Sunday afternoon from the coffee table,
And was sometimes seen once again when it would be brought
From the stacks of paper in the coal bin to be thrust hopefully
Through the furnace door and stuffed under the reluctant coals.

She hasn't got away from DeSantis yet. Her name was on his
Desk today and in his talk.
Such a circling back. After a long time of being aware of
Him in our home, tonight at last he is aware of her in his.

35.

I dreamt I died at the age of three
And went to Heaven,
And that as I was lounging near the throne,
On the seat of a red fire engine, actually,
Both its doors open, with a thousand grownups milling
Around, but quietly,
I saw a large man dressed all in white approach alone;
He wore a rainbow-colored tie, his face and hands
Were long and weathered, and I knew
That he was loud although he hadn't spoken;
He winked and smiled at me and I saw
That he was my Uncle Ed.
Then I noticed that he carried a black toolbox
With a broken lock, and that his black shoes had white laces.
We all watched him walk up to God
And it took him a long time, and when he got to God

He put his toolbox and his trombone down and leaned close;
Casually then, in a disarming way, as though
He were at a party, and reaching
For his cigarettes on the shelf, he said to God:
"Tell me all about Yourself."

36.

A common assumption
Is that our ascension into Heaven
Will be a mingling thing,
A great elated buoyant throng winging
Virtuously commingled headlong through a dazzling portal
Into whatever sort of place Heaven is,
There to move about in whatever amorphous state God
    ordains,
Searching then in sun or mist for others
That we loved or if that took too long, seeking out
A list of the blissfully rewarded, or better, seeing
Those names slid to us beneath our stateroom, cabin,
Cottage door; the emphasis in any case on togetherness,
Association, participation.

Here on earth, meanwhile, there are good people, saintly even,
I don't care much for nor they for me; therefore must I
Love everyone in Heaven just because they're good
And just because I should?
What of loners like Thoreau? Could he keep
At arm's, wing's, vapor's length all those who wanted
To walk, glide, seep, flit over, and talk? And what if he
Could not abide the place and decided to call it quits?
Would he vanish without a trace? Or would he be obliged,
Once there, to hang on, glumly noting heavenly flora,
Writing little bits, trying out new terrain, and
Nibbling, absorbing, inhaling the celestial
Wild plum.

The question consumes me because I'm going there eventually,
Not being nearly bad enough for hell (I've never personally
    known anyone
So thoroughly evil as to merit that drastic fate); I see,
Though, that the only thing to do is wait. We'll each of us
Know on some distant date, won't we, unless you happen
To believe in oblivion, in which case
An obliging God may grant you your belief.

And speaking of God — how happy can He be, looking on
While His human race weakly, coldly, sadly fails?
And if God in Heaven is not happy,
As He could not, cannot be,
Then I needn't be concerned about who I'll like there,
And who'll like me,
And sticking it out together
Through all eternity.

37.

Don Cataldo and Fallon
And some of the other guys and I
Had an idea to ride our bikes to
Eastwood Park and take our lunches
And ride the rides there.
It was my idea, in fact, and I gloried
In their warm response and I
Rode home whistling.

The day came dark and heavy, warm
And cheerless. The radio predicted rain.
My mother said I couldn't go.
"I planned it, Mom. They're waiting for me."
She was adamant. Cataldo and the others
Came looking for me. I went out on the front porch

And said I'd decided not to go.
"It looks like rain," I said.
They urged me to take a chance.
"We're all set," they said.
I looked wisely at the sky and said I thought
We'd better not.
I sat on the steps and watched them angrily ride off.

Soon the rain came.
It fell long and hard.
Before they got there they were soaked.
Never again were we ever really close.
My mother had been right about the rain,
But they had been soaked together.

38.

The dogs of the forties, the dogs of Detroit;
Terriers of all sorts, mostly, as varied and mongrelized
As their owners, just as yippy but more alert.
Here and there a chow, a collie, a feared German shepherd
(Usually owned by a feared German), a couple of
Grave boxers and a scattering of setters, all benign and loose.
Our first dog was named Tippy, Tippy the First,
As it turned out.
More black and more terrier than anything else, with
White and light brown on his face and paws, he was a happy
    pup,
Licking my face and falling asleep in the basement one night
In the snug and scented confines of my father's shoe.
I had never seen anything so perfect. We spent hours together.
I took him on long, rambling walks, carrying him home half
Inside my jacket. We rolled in the grass, nuzzling one
    another,
And studied each other with steadfast curiosity.
There was something about him that bothered my mother,
    however,

For she warned us daily what would
Happen unless certain things
Were done or not done, the first by us, the second by Tip.
Life was full of warnings then, but the name "Humane Society"
Became a dreaded image; in dreams I saw white trucks race up
On unsuspecting dogs, two or three men jump out and throw
Nets, pitch the dogs inside, race off, a bell clanging,
Drowning the worry and whine of the dogs, one of them
    mine.
But that is all it was, a dream —
I had never seen one of their trucks
Or one of their men, and never would.

But I came home from school one warm day at lunchtime,
    when Tippy
Was six months old. I looked in the basement for him.
He wasn't there.
My mother was in the kitchen.
"Hi, Mom," I said. "Where's Tip? He's not downstairs."
She concentrated on the sandwich she was fixing for me,
Cutting it carefully into halves.
"I warned you," she said. "I warned you what would happen,
But nobody pays any attention to me."
We both stared at the sandwich.
I was afraid to speak.
She went to the refrigerator, uncapped a bottle of milk,
Poured the cream into a small blue pitcher.
"Is Tippy gone?" I asked.
"Yes."
"Where?"
"The Humane Society took him."
I said, "Oh," as though I had expected it
And could understand it.
I quickly went through the living room to the stairs, went up
To the bathroom, closed the door, and sat on the toilet.

I don't remember doing that. I don't remember anything until
The door opened and I saw her standing there.
She looked at me
As I sat there, my hands clasped, my head down, my mouth
open;
Tears ran into my mouth and dropped off my chin onto my
legs.
Then she was on her knees in front of me.
"Geraldy, Geraldy," she said in an agony. "I told you
What would happen! I told you!"
I nodded and wept.
She held my shoulders.
We stayed that way a long time.
Once I sobbed, "Tippy's gone."
And that was the end of our first dog.

As years passed there were others —
Another Tippy, who died early and was buried
By my father in a shallow hole behind the garage and covered
With maple leaves and earth while my brother and sister
and I
Silently grieved;
A third Tippy, who lasted, who had several litters,
Who did not like anyone much, whose fur was flinty as her
Personality, but whom we humored along halfheartedly
Until the winter night, feeling even crustier than usual,
She went into the street ignoring Carl's call and was killed
By a blue DeSoto that wasn't going fast but didn't stop;
And our last dog, Blotto, Tippy's daughter, the best of the best,
A combination of beauty, spirit, and
Warmth, who belonged to us
And mostly to me between the time I was eleven and
seventeen,
Who waited at the edges of all the ball games, at the doors of
All the drugstores, who delivered papers with me, who could

Outrun dogs twice her size, who could hear my whistle blocks
Away and always came when I called, and who told me over
  and over
That I was someone special.

For several years we had both Blotto and her mother
And one spring they both had litters; for a while we
Owned fifteen dogs, but never again
Did my mother threaten one of them, or me.
One bitter cold high school day I came home to find Blotto
  gone.
I whistled again in the after-supper dark and again at ten,
But she did not appear.
At seven the next morning I crunched through the new snow,
Calling, and I found her in the alley, standing motionless
By the Vanadia's garage. I called to her at a little distance,
But she shivered and did not come. I carried her to our garage
And put her down at the door of her doghouse
And she went in.
There was a spot of blood on her tail. She lay down
With her nose out the door as always and looked at me and I
Heard her tail thump.

I called at noon from school and my mother said Blotto was
  dead.

In the glow of the afternoon's low red sun I trudged to
The garage. Her back was to the door.
It was hard to get her out.
I was appalled at her stiffness;
Once I had her out I did not touch her again.
Carol Ann came out to the garage, gave me a questioning
  look;
Then we stood near Blotto and turned our blurring eyes
Away from each other.

The dogs of childhood, rounding off the families,
Harbingers of love and distant sorrow,
Fillers of the chinks in lives and houses,
They link a child to things he needs to know.

39.

I came up the driveway to the side door in
Deep November's suppertime dark;
I had run all the way home from St. Philip's field
Throwing the football underhand as high
As the highest branches and far enough ahead
To never break stride;
I was flushed, rough, hot in the sweater,
I was thirteen, tireless, bursting . . .

No sound from the lace-curtained kitchen window brightly
    above;
I went in softly and stood on the basement landing, listening;
Voices from the dining room! I was late!
I crept up the steps to the kitchen door,
Opened it, and stared warily, guiltily at my gathered family —
But what was this? Tranquillity. No bawling out.
No threats, nothing. Her face completely calm.
"Wash your hands," was all she said.

I did. And took my place, my napkin from its ring,
And ravenously, deliriously, a helping of everything.

40.

Ralph Smith and I used to sit on the porch and talk
About things like if Christ were to return
As some were predicting
How would He look?
Would He assume the garb of the period, as before?

That means no robe. No sandals, except
Perhaps on summer weekends.
We thought no beard, but chances are better now.
How would He be accepted in a broadcloth shirt,
Double-breasted suit and support hose?
Would the suit have seams?
Wait, though — if He went into carpentry again it means
Work pants, construction boots, and a T-shirt, depending
Of course on whether He could get into the union.
Wait, wait, wait — wouldn't He be a priest, black suit,
    vestments?
No. He couldn't be a priest. He'd have to be the Pope. But
If He arrived and announced: "God is a Catholic," what effect
Would that have on everyone?
What if He proved beyond doubt
That He was God and He said,
"Yes, I'm a Catholic," and He said that
The Moslems and Hindus and
Lutherans and Baptists better join or else
They're out of the picture?
Somehow that didn't sound like Him.
What if He said it didn't make any difference what religion
    you were?
Ralph and I weren't sure He'd say that either.
Complex problems, endless ramifications.
We wished He would come back,
But we didn't see how He could.

41.

Opa died when I was fifteen
And when we got to Conestogo he had been dressed
In his dark blue velvet clerical gown and starched
White linen befkins, and they had parted his beard
The way he kept it, the tapering tips reaching along

82

Past where the pleats began.
They had put the casket in the music room in the place
Where the small bed had been and where he said his
Last words, which were to Oma: *"Du komm auch."*
It means, "You are coming too," and partly because
I did not know the depth of his belief the words
Sounded threatening to me; to my elders, however,
It was a profession of faith and a final cry of love.

He died at noon on Friday, October 5th, 1945.
We gathered there, the three families, and with
My cousins home from the war and my brother not yet
Gone, it was to be the only time we would all be
In Conestogo at once.
We wandered about, unused to each other
There, and huddled silently in the kitchen by the stove.

Uncle Stan chose to sleep, and drink, it was said, down
At the Trail's End Hotel; I was assigned to a cot
In the attic where I lay under ancient chest-scented
Woolens and dry rafters, listening to a spasmodic wind
Whip at mulberry limbs and tear at the spruce trees
That sighed in summer, and quiver the small panes of
Glass at my head that allowed me a view
Below of a moonlit blue pump and the dancing grass.

The evening before the funeral my mother suddenly did
What I knew instantly I had been dreading: she flung
Herself at the casket screaming and sobbing a name
Out of childhood she had for her father.
Embarrassed but not really surprised, I watched with
My wide-eyed cousins through a doorway as they held
Her and I remember their urgent whispers, Aunt Jo's
Soft pleading, Uncle Stan's louder: "Frieda, for

God's sake, there are children here!" and her
Turning on him in a fury: "I loved him! You didn't!"
Then Oma was there with a sharp, "Friedchen!" and
My mother sat down and began to cry softly.

Later I heard that during the previous winter
Uncle Stan, in an ill-tempered patriotic fit,
Had refused to allow German to be spoken in his home
When Opa and Oma, too old to endure the hardship of
A Conestogo winter, had been staying there.
I wondered what part that played in Opa's refusal
To get out of bed that day in September as the
Time to leave for Detroit approached. He had been his
Own master too long, and the thought of being
Transported out of his domain once again, to be
Helped in and out of chairs and cars, to be ordered,
Advised, shunted, and ignored was enough, possibly,
To decide him, tired as he was, on the other trip.

The funeral was held at St. Matthew's Evangelical
Lutheran Church on Monday at 2:30 P.M.,
Reverend Mosig officiating.
    Come, ye disconsolate, where'er ye languish,
    Come to the mercy-seat, fervently kneel;
    Here bring your wounded hearts, here tell your anguish,
    Earth has no sorrow that Heaven cannot heal.
I had never seen the little church filled with people;
I had been up the stairs to ring the bells, and other
Times, drowsy afternoons, I would wander about the village,
Chance upon the church, slip inside, sit and
Look around and watch the sun glow and fade and watch a
Bumblebee bump along a wall. But that was all.
    Lord, now lettest Thou Thy servant depart in
    peace according to Thy word, for mine eyes
    have seen Thy salvation.

I looked at my mother; she seemed composed, even serene.
There would not be another scene, not today.

I saw Eddie Veitel, a river, barn, and field friend; he
Looked at me and raised his eyebrows comically; how odd
To see him here and now.
      Now dear mourners our dear Christian brother, the
      Reverend Holm, was a lover of gardens; we know that
      wherever he was he planted a garden. In his first
      parish in North Easthope he planted a beautiful
      garden, and trees which he planted in his time
      are still standing and have grown well.
My hurriedly purchased new black shoes began to hurt.
      And so Reverend Holm went to study at the University
      in Kiel, and it was natural science, and later on
      he became a student of spiritual science, and still
      later at the seminary in Kropp; and this, my dear
      Christian friends, shows that he was not satisfied
      with natural science, but he looked for spiritual
      science, and he became a minister of the Saviour,
      Jesus Christ, the redeemer of our souls.
I looked around for Marty and Charley. I had
Never seen them wearing suits.

      We have come now to that time and to that
      hour and we who are looking on,
      like the people who looked
      on the burial of Jacob in that long distant past, we
      see a family put into the chosen place the mortal remains
      of their father and we are looking on, and we see your
      love and your respect for him. Not only are we looking,
      but when you go away we will
      mark that place and remember
      it, for truly, we say, "Here lie the mortal remains of a
      man who loved his family and

who was loved by his family,
a man of God."

Mostly I watched Oma's face as they lowered Opa into the
    earth;
It was set, severe, almost angry, but her eyes were distant,
As though she were brooding on other days.
The wind blew the folds of her black coat.
Curled yellow leaves sailed out of the maple above the grave.
They had been together fifty-five years.
Oma said later she would gladly
Have died the same day. She had eleven years to wait,
And all the winters were in Detroit.
I learned that day that all marriages end sadly.

42.

Somewhere in the country,
Rusting maybe in a cluster of junkyard sheet metal
Next to the highway that runs out the poor side of town,
Lie the remains of a tan 1946 Plymouth coupe;
It had an outside sun visor and a chrome tailpipe piece.
Inside it smelled of Old Spice and gardenia corsages;
It was my first car.

The National Bank of Detroit and I
Paid nine hundred and fifty
For it in 1949; I washed and waxed it behind our garage
And on Saturday nights it would transport Barbara Barrett
And me along blackly shining streets while I gazed out
Through slowly clacking wipers at the gratifying bead-sized
Raindrops on the glistening hood.
It was a quiet car and ran well and we were cozy inside;
Night air poured through the vent balmy and lake fresh.
We went to movies like *Unfaithfully Yours,* with
Rex Harrison and Linda Darnell, ordered cheeseburgers at
    Cupid's,

Were vaguely aware of Vaughn Monroe and his orchestra
Doing "Dance, Ballerina, Dance"; then we moved slowly
Along Charlevoix and midnight-empty Alter Road
To her Ashland Avenue door down in the river fog and mist.
Under a streetlight's high glare and with the sound of lake
Freighter foghorns coming out of the dripping trees, we would
Arrive at her porch, where Barbara, intelligent and spirited,
But moody, might or might not kiss me, a disposition which
Made her touch a curiosity and her charity memorable.

It had been in winter, on dry gray Sunday afternoons
That I had learned to drive. My father sat peacefully
Beside me, a cigar in his teeth, gloved hands in his lap,
Smiling, saying, "That's right. Now you've got it."
He was a good teacher but I took the test too soon.
When the officer slid in beside me I switched on the lights.
"What are you doing?" he asked. "It's two o'clock
In the afternoon." I agreed and turned them off.
After a while he said, in resigned but kindly tones,
"This is your ignition here."
I drove us away from the curb, shifting deftly from
First to third. We crawled around the block and
Returned without incident. He considered his forms,
Glanced at me thoughtfully, and at last passed me
And got out, looking back once, apprehensively.
A year later I was driving a dump truck for a construction
Firm, wondering sometimes what could have been so baffling,
This simple skill that gave me so much pleasure now.

Weeks and months flocked by with me floating home at night
On a sea of radio waves, scent of a smooth throat and cheek
Clouding my head; I would open the side door, all quickness
And stealth, supporting the weight of the door with my own
To eliminate its lonely squeak; I drank milk leaning against
The refrigerator door, feeling strong, rich, and grown.

Upstairs I would lie in bed, hear my parents' door creak,
Follow my mother's footsteps to the bathroom.
I looked down from the window at my car, heard
The soft snaps of its settling sounds.

Once I asked my mother why she had never learned
To drive. She dismissed the notion with a scornful laugh.
The thought had never occurred to her, she said,
And never would.
I told her she was missing something really good.

43.

I visited Mrs. Wasek down on Alter Road this afternoon;
We sat in her kitchen, she fixed coffee, and we talked of the
    past:
"It makes me so happy you and Arthur was always such good
    friends."
She is small, good-humored, white-haired, and gently spoken.
Her Latvian accent is as palatable to the ear as her pancakes
Are to the tongue; delicate as a poppy petal,
She worked the night shift
At Dodge for fifteen years.
Art is her only child and when we
Were grade-schoolers she worried
About whether or not he would have friends. As it turned out,
The comfort and hospitality of her house
Made it the headquarters
Of a group that ranged up to a dozen or more, through high
    school, military and college years,
And for some, long after that.
Pancakes after Sunday mass was a ritual, sometimes just Art
    and me,
Sometimes Hulber and Scanlon too, and some of the others.
Art was not a churchgoer in those years, and he would sleep

Until someone woke him, and he would wake up laughing,
and chortle
Throughout the day. Art loved movies, engineering, and
music;
He dined with flourishes, was intense
In his loyalties. After devouring the pancakes (one cup flour,
One cup milk, four eggs, a little sugar, pinch of salt) and
plenty of strong, hot coffee,
We sank deep into armchairs, feet up, to
Drowse and mumble through a few balmy
Hours of Mozart, Beethoven,
Dvořák and Brahms.
It was a kingly and carefree time in Detroit then, and the
Alter Road
Hours at Art's were particularly agreeable; for them
We had in large part Art's mother to thank.

"I am so sorry to hear about your mother," she says now.
"I don't see her except one time when you and Art was little.
I remember Art when he come home he say your mother is so
strict."
She lives in the spotless house alone now. Art's father,
Who used to tell us stories
We could not understand because his
Laugh was so robust and his voice
So Russian, who used to pass
Beaming through the dining room and with a wink and an
approving nod
Say, "Eat'm up, fellas," died sternly coughing in the bedroom
Five years ago.
"It was so nice, those days when all you boys was here," Mrs.
Wasek says.

When I left I drove up Alter, turned left at Charlevoix —
My old way home.

My mother used to be jealous.
"Mrs. Wasek, Mrs. Wasek, that's all
I hear," she complained one Sunday upon my return.
Art and the others
Would come over to my house too, but just for a beer, and
It wasn't the same.
The DeSantis Funeral Home is on the
Corner of Chalmers; I pulled up
Alongside it at a red light. A few dry leaves, clattering
Lightly along the sidewalk, held for a moment in weedy spears
That grew out of a crack between the walk and the wall, then
    drifted on.
On the other side of the wall my mother lay.
I thought about parking and going in to see her, but all of us
Were due back at four, and perhaps she wasn't ready yet.
To ring the doorbell now and ask for her
Seemed childish and might have proved embarrassing if futile.
She would have appreciated the gesture, though.
I looked at my watch. There wasn't time.
There were things to do and I had visited too long.
The light changed.
It felt all wrong, but I slowly drove away.
Beyond the red brick wall I saw my mother in her casket
Despondently wave her arm.
"Mrs. Wasek, Mrs. Wasek," I heard her say.

44.

We've received the death certificate.
Near the bottom I read:
> CAUSE OF DEATH: ARTERIOSCLEROTIC HEART
> DISEASE

So now there was a death certificate
To place in a large envelope

With her birth certificate;
One to certify that she had been born,
The other that she had died.
Just those two. No third
To indicate
That she had lived.

45.

It is almost time to go to the funeral home.
My father, dreading this moment, has had several drinks
In the kitchen. Someone gave him a tranquilizer and he took
    that too.
Now he sits nervously on the sofa; his eyes, wide
And wounded, dart rapidly about the living room.
A few neighbors try to talk to him.
My sister and her husband Roy arrive. They go to him,
Hold his hands, ask if everything is all right.
He nods, says softly, "Yes. I'm okay." He doesn't look
Directly at anyone. His dark blue suit
Is dusty on the shoulders and the sleeves are too long.

In DeSantis's parking lot he won't get out of the car.
His eyes are almost shut and he clutches the edge of the seat.
In an anguished voice he says: "Where are my keys?
Somebody took my keys." Roy and I look at each other.
Roy is slight, wiry, his manner confident and kind.
He says, "Dad, do you know where you are?" My father nods.
"Do you know what we're here for?" My father nods again.
He collects himself then, his eyes open and focus, and he says:
"Yes. Yes." We ease him out of the car and go inside.

He does not want to go immediately into the room where she
    lies.
"I need to rest a minute," he says, and we lead him to a
    bench.

DeSantis comes over, looking no different from when I was a
    boy.
"How is he?" he whispers.
"Not good."
Roy says, "He's pretty wobbly."
"He'll be all right," DeSantis says, looking over at my father.

Carl and his wife Ruth arrive. They have their five children
With them. I kiss the solemn, bright, and beautiful girls,
Shake hands with the boys. "Tonight is Halloween,"
Young Vincent breathes intensely. "We're going trick or
    treating."

With Carl on my father's left and I on the right, we go into
The room. It is a long room and I see her at the far end.
We cross the room slowly. My father's eyes, rimmed with
    tears,
Are riveted on the coffin; the muscles in his face ripple,
Like a horse shaking flies; at last we are there.
We gaze down at her for a long time.
I remember her lying on the sofa like this. She looks all right,
Except that the corners of her mouth are drawn down. She
    seems angry.
I wonder if they couldn't have done something about that.
My second thought is that it doesn't make any difference.
The overpowering smell of flowers
Is worse. I remember why I hate a florist shop.
Shelves of cold
White roses, a wall of orchids, these smells mean death.
I keep searching her face, remembering other recent
    long-distance
And anguished words: "Something's not right!" and beginning
    to cry.
"What, Mom? What's not right?"
"I don't know! But something's not right!"

Only two weeks ago? She had sensed it coming.
It was the only time
I ever heard her sound afraid.
And still I watch, trying to bring those eyes to life,
Simply to recall, if I can, how
She looked and sounded when she said
Something, anything; but nothing comes.
I am conscious of being
Self-conscious.

My father reaches out suddenly. His hand is on her forearm.
He holds her tightly, now near the wrist, now up toward the
    elbow.
He watches her face, and he squeezes.
We let him and finally he gives up.
Calmer now, he says: "She was a good woman. She was a
    very fine woman."
Someone else says: "She had a good long life. She was, what,
    seventy-six?"
"The way things are," someone else says, "that's longer than
    we'll get."

Later the room is filled with relatives, neighbors, some people
I don't know. I see my father laughing with some men from
    Parke Davis.
Uncle Rim and Aunt Verna have arrived. He has had a stroke
And is using a cane.
Aunt Irma is there without Uncle Harold. "He couldn't
    come," she says,
Sadly smiling. "Harold has cancer, you know. Left lung."
She continues to smile, her face a mask.
Uncle Harold had been a policeman, sometimes driving his
    patrol car
By our house for a midday visit. He was tall, lean, broad-
    shouldered,

And handsome, with black wavy hair and light blue eyes.
His voice was tough and friendly and of all my boyhood
    heroes,
He was the only one I really knew. When he had driven
    away,
I would tell everyone, "That was my uncle."
His name used to be in the papers:
        Patrolman Harold Dumas shot and captured
        a thief in an alley near St. Jean and Mack
        last night. The victim, who admitted holding
        up an A&P store earlier, is hospitalized
        with a fractured elbow.
"We have a trailer in Jacksonville now," Aunt Irma is saying.
"We're going to try and get him down there next month."

My mother's sister came in. I kissed her and said, "Hello,
    Aunt Jo."
I hadn't realized before how similar their voices were.
At the coffin she stared at the determined expression
While I tried to imagine their linked years: Country
Children before the century turned,
Nurses in Philadelphia, then
Forty years wives and mothers together.
At length she said, "So she's the first."
Still looking at my mother
She said to me, "You know, we were
Engaged the same day. We both
Got our rings in Uncle Stan's car, on a Sunday ride out to
    Frankfort."
I didn't hear the question someone whispered on the other
    side,
But I heard Aunt Jo's reply: "No, no, she was spunky.
She was spunky as they come."
A few more seconds passed. Then Aunt Jo leaned over
And kissed my mother's forehead.
"Auf Wiedersehen, Schwesterlein," she softly said.

46.

Here are four aged snapshots
Spread across two pages whose edges are curled and ripped;
Beneath them a title
In her script:
An   Afternoon   in   Waterloo   Park
It is July, 1917.
Two snapshots are sunny, two shaded by a cloud.
It was a breezy day, you can see the pale turned-up
Undersides of leaves.
She and Jo are home, on leave from their Philadelphia wards:
With them are their brother Reimer, called Rim now,
His intended bride, Verna, and a young man named Bert.
My mother wears an ankle-length dress, a wide straw hat,
And as she sits laughing atop the cannon you can see
Her striped stockings and shining shoes with double straps.
There is tumbling on the grass, dancing beneath the trees,
Poses struck beside a chair on a rough wood platform
(BAND CONCERT 8 P.M.) on the broad deserted grass.
They have fallen now or jumped or have been pushed; they
Collapse in helpless shrieks; there is touching, sprawling,
Stretching, faces raised to the sun.
Rim and Bert wear trim dark suits, vests, starched collars,
Straw boaters. But where are other people? Is it Saturday?
Sunday? Why can no one else be seen across that wide
And sweeping green? Here Bert watches my mother with a
Tender smile; he helps her onto the cannon, holding her
Right forearm, holding her where my father held her
In love and anguish standing by the casket fifty-one years
     later.
Their smiles are affectionate and the laughter must have gone
Through the trees out to King Street and someone passing
     must have
Heard them happy and blooming in the park that day.
She clowned and climbed and ran and rested on the grass and

Inhaled the evergreen air; if Bert desired her,
She did not respond. She had no regrets as yet and nothing
    hurt.
She was twenty-five.
It was a time to dance in Waterloo Park,
A day to play
And be alive.

47.

Messiah Lutheran Church has not changed much.
It may not have changed at all since I as a small boy
Accompanied my mother to Sunday services here.
An artist's copy of the Last Supper with Christ looking
More drowsy than serene still looms behind the gaunt white
Head of Reverend Loeber, whose external modifications
Are also slight.

One Sunday they were singing the doxology at the end of the
Service and my mother leaned down to listen to me. Instead
    of
"Praise Father, Son and Holy Ghost," I piped, "Praise
Father, Son and home we go."
Outside on the sidewalk she told people about it. I was
    abashed,
But she smiled down and laughed and seemed proud of me.

We leave the open casket and take places in the third pew.
Relatives and friends arrive, go to the front, pray
Or try to pray, turn, glance at us, sit behind us.

The sermon is all right. Loeber is eloquent, fervent,
A bit dramatic. It is a finely honed performance, reminding
Believers of what it is they believe in,
Telling us that she believed it too
And saying with conviction that all of it is true.

Words of comfort and reinforcement. It is what we expect,
It is what he should do, it is the only thing he can do.

Loeber has known my mother
For almost forty years; he speaks
Briefly of her devout belief.
He had sat beside her bed at home
And had been with her in hospitals. He knew her well.
But it is hard to picture her discussing theology,
Telling Loeber what she thinks concerning Heaven and Hell.

Before we came in I wondered
If my throat would tighten, my eyes
Blur, my nose give me away, and finally, once, they do.
It was not the music, or prayers to God to lead her by her
Child's hand, nor can any of Loeber's fine
And rolling phrases lay a claim;
It was only the simple final mention of her name.

48.

The long line leaves for Mount Olivet; heavily,
Importantly, we glide through stoplights.
People in cars, on porches, stare at the hearse
And somberly study our exposed faces.
My father sits beside me.
We watch the casket jiggle gently over bumps.

DeSantis races back and forth; where we go,
Life freezes. Faces mirror ours,
And hers; all is acquiescence, she takes precedence,
Drivers grip their wheels and wait, blankly,
Patiently, tamely, as if to say,
"We'll let her have her way
This one last time."

We pass Chandler Park where Raymond Leslie and John Peck
And I went to play ball all day on my tenth birthday.
We rode our bikes a mile to get there, with three lunches
She made tucked in my basket, and money for big bottles
Of cream soda snug in my pocket. Later the park was one of
The places my father chose for driving lessons; now
He doesn't seem to notice the park or the people;
He stares ahead, his eyes dull, quiet, and dry.
A funeral is a tense series of anticlimaxes.

As we approach the cemetery I see a man
On the sidewalk. He stops when he sees the hearse, turns,
Faces the street. He is perhaps sixty, has the red cheek and
Long head of an Irish farmer; his shirt is white, his suit
Baggy, his tie knotted large.
He puts his feet together and comes to rapt attention;
Then with his mournful eye on my mother's casket he sweeps
His hat off and holds it against his breast as we go by.
He stays that way till we turn in the gate.

We did not stand beside the grave and see her lowered;
We left her in a chapel. They would wait till we were gone
To bury her. At the church they led us up an aisle
And down a hall while they closed the lid; they think
To cushion us from too much finality,
While we busily imagine what we do not see.

49.

Back at the house we crowd each other close
And spill out into the yard,
All of us, her husband, daughter, sons,
Her brother, sister, nieces, nephews,
Their wives and husbands and children;
She too is here in a way, the ghost hostess
At her last party.

We eat the ham, the salad, the cake,
Catch up on each other, years since we've
Been together like this.
The neighbor women work efficiently in the kitchen,
A child cries in the side drive, an anxious moment
In the living room when Uncle Rim's face goes white
And he leans forward in the rocker trying to breathe —
Reg's wife Jean, a nurse, is called; she kneels before him,
Takes the plate from his lap. The spell passes
And soon there is laughter out among the sunlit yellow
Leaves in back; running games start up in front.

We are done with sadness.
About my mother little is said.
We are gobbling, galloping, gossiping,
Very happy to be not among the dead.

        50.

Here are three pictures come somehow together side
By side; the first is a portrait of my mother
At three and a half, standing dim and distant
In yellow tan tints beside a chair
In Baumann's Photography Studio in Buffalo, New York;
The second shows her standing outside on a gray stool
At the front windows of the Dickerson house; she is
Aproned and gloved and in her seventies, planting
Coleus in a green flower box;
The third has her in the Conestogo churchyard cemetery
Beside Opa's grave. The stone in the sun is blinding white
And topped by a cross; it reaches almost to the short sleeve
Of her checked cotton dress. She stands stiffly, and squints.
It is not, this last picture, a view of her
Beneath a maple, beside a grave. It is a picture
Of her and her father. Opa, in shadows, is understood.
He took her to the photographers in 1894 to keep alive

The child who ran through the house calling, "Papa, Papa,
Wo bist Du?" he planted fifty gardens and lived long enough
To see the girl grow to middle age and come along
Planting gardens of her own, he lies there at her foot
In St. Matthew's rich earth, firm in the belief
That he will sprout again.

Two hundred miles back this way she now lies low
In her own last flowery bed, while I sleepily turn pages
And watch the slowly speeding growing sinking
Ever-posing lives go by.

Soon solemn snapshots will be taken by her grave
With attendant stiffened flights: If autumn comes
Can ice be far behind?
The human race, hurrying, needs the camera for a clear
View of the blurry pace; hating to leave,
And leaving,
Cherishing daughters, moments, visions,
We cry, smile, snap the shutter, try
To perpetuate and touch and watch and keep
Our elusive loves.

51.

Out of these hundreds of snapshots
There are few of her smiling — but here is one.
It is 1951. She is sixty, I am newly twenty-one,
On leave, and we have come again to Conestogo,
Where we stand laughing in the August sun in the side
    garden.
Opa has been dead six years, Oma will die in five.
We have our arms around each other,
My mother and I, my hand
On the fleshy bulge where her corset stops,
Hers on my starched and sun-bleached khaki shirt.

She looks so very happy, her eyes and smile too genuine
For just the camera's purpose, which as I say
She never did in any case. The air blew sweetly at us
While she roamed again with Oma,
Speaking German in kitchen
And garden, remembering old things and acting young.

Her happiness there. It maybe matched my own.
My twenty summers there all told me that this was a place
Of placid talk, gentle bedtimes,
Soft murmurs from my parents'
Bedroom, and cool night Canadian breezes that washed my
    brown cheek
And further comforted her clear and gentled mind.
I never worried about her there — her thoughts were outward
    turned,
And so therefore were mine, and my father's, I suppose;
The hours, noon or midnight, were slowed in light repose.
And if any man or woman
I chanced upon the whole day long, in
Barn or garden, field or road,
Was stopped up with envy, malice,
Greed or hate, I never knew it —
They fooled the boy I was with
Long and quiet laughter and warming eyes;
And when I ran home
To Opa and Oma's, pushed through the creaking gate,
Moving boughs above me whispered
That Conestogo's country magic continued inside the house —
Trouble to come, if any,
Could wait.

    52.

Why do I sit here?
Why ponder, write these notes,

Think on her, turn the pages of her life,
Study her changing face?
I wrote trivial letters to her while she lived:
    "Hello, Mom, how are you, I am fine,
    not much new, say hello to all for me."
Not a trace of anything truly felt that I recall,
Everything small, small, the news, trite actions
Of the mundane day, my leaden mind when writing
Light-years away.

Her letters were the same;
    "The weather not as hot today.
    Uncle Stan is worse."
I read them twice, three times, not knowing
What I wanted her to say. We were terse with each other,
We knew no other way.
And so I sit and scribble marks on paper that presume to say
How it was then, how things were with her.
What a futile thing,
To try to make her live again.

53.

My father and I have walked down to the corner
Here this morning for nine o'clock mass at St. Philip's.
I did not hold his arm too much, but he is still shaky
And had to be careful on the sidewalk where the
Elm roots have lifted and tilted squares, places
I on roller skates used to lightly leap.

It is a different St. Philip Neri church; the one I
Knew so well is the gymnasium now.
The new church, plain, large, and none too beautiful,
Sprawls across our old football lot. The pew we sit in
Is on the spot where I caught touchdown passes when I

Ran straight and fast for the goal line — the sidewalk —
Faked, then cut left.

The priest has delivered a heartfelt but boring sermon
Which does not touch our lives this morning at all.
He might just as well have stood there softly
Calling, "Hut hut hut."
I don't know if he is faking, or what he is throwing,
Or which way he is going to cut.

54.

I wonder how many people in this church believe in God.
Really believe.
Half? Three-quarters? The same proportions, perhaps,
As for all people everywhere
Outside these walls.
Faith, hope, reason, and the easiest of these is reason.
One believes in the existence of man, in
The intricacies of his body and brain, one believes
In the fine balance between animal and plant,
One believes in the water cycle,
In the scope of earth, sun, stars, universe,
One believes in the mathematical possibilities of other beings
In other worlds, and sometimes one believes that
The planning had a Planner.

And what is true of what the Planner wants of you and me?
We do not agree on that. There are conflicting thoughts.
He has hidden Himself to such a degree that men have
    fought,
Slaughtered each other over how they think He
Would like them to order the daily details of their littered
    lives.

It was in high school that I grumbled: If He wants us to do
Certain things in certain ways, why not tell us straight out,
Rather than rely on intermediaries (who may be only half-
   listening)
To relay the message? And which intermediary shall we listen
   to,
Disagreeing as they do?
Has the message as it's been passed been garbled,
Due to mumbling?

Little has come through clearly, unless you count the Ten
Commandments, and they don't cover all the possibilities.
(I once thought that they would have been adhered to
More closely all these years if, instead of having been
Delivered privately to Moses, they had been blasted
One afternoon in full view of multitudes into the side of
Mt. Sinai in letters eighty cubits high,
And had continued to be visible
Glowing eerily in blue ever since at night.)

In the meantime there exists among believers
A bothersome mist of fine confusion here;
So a lot of people are simply being kind
And figure to play the rest of it by ear.

55.

The nuns of St. Philip's have modified their habits somewhat,
In line with the loosening times;
You can see their ankles now and the hair on their heads.
A mystery is gone, that measured tread
And heightened dignity is no longer there.
I think we admired their willpower as we eyed
Their shielded cheeks and heavy clothes
On spring and summer afternoons.

We wondered how they stood it, how so many
Could be sweet-tempered in temperatures like those.
We tried to figure out which ones became nuns
Because they were going bald.
In every Catholic school one nun is singled
Out as being truly bald.
Jimmy Hamil said he had seen old Sister Margaret Mary
Tumble down the convent's back porch steps and that
Before she had adjusted things he had seen
Her shining bare head.
She did have a hairless look about her,
So we believed him.
Now nuns let their hair show. They seem more comfortable,
Less formidable, and we see that there is no mystery,
No secret after all.
Except old Sister Margaret Mary —
She probably really was bald.

56.

Shall I believe
That the space between and beyond racing stars
Goes on and on, ever spreading, bending,
Widening, never ending?

Thoughtful men have lived who felt they knew,
Who believed it to be true
And having gone that far
Went on and believed in God who goes on and on too,
Who never began,
Who'll never end.
Finding no alternative to that first-mentioned mystery
They saw nothing foolish about the second
Or any of the others.

So here's another topic my mother
Never touched on with me
Or anyone else in the family;
We stayed down on the ground with one another
While any flights of fancy I had were taken with friends.
What fun to roam it might have been
Inside the home.

57.

I went to Carstens School today
To inhale the happy halls and
Look around and see what still was true
Of the time when I was there and call
On whoever might be there that I once knew.
Few graduates come back, apparently,
And in Miss Maher's office the new old ladies
Seemed pleased and mildly astonished
At my interest. They allowed me to wander
Alone and in the corridors I stared at floor
Mosaics, radiators and varnished rails that I had
Owned and as I saw them owned again.

Over thirty years have passed since the second
Grade's Mrs. Ellis taught me to subtract with
Some thoughtful business about a house and its
Basement, but there she was, looking much the same,
As did Mrs. Schneider, who in gym bloomers
Demonstrated one afternoon on the south playground
The art of hitting shoulder-high pitches
Every bit as far as the more reachable sort.
They remembered me, these two, but not without effort,
And after a brief exchange they left the old days,
And the future, to me.

Miss Mahoney is gone, a principal now in another school;
Miss Ireland has retired; Miss Cane has died.
The dreaded Miss Edgerton is gone too, I did not
Ask where. Immense, brute-strong Miss Edgerton,
With her black-banged hair chopped short in back
Revealing her squat neck, furiously flinging her keys
The length of the room to crack against the blackboard,
Who held us under the chin with her iron fingers,
Who stood me up and called me a four-flusher, a term
I had never heard but instantly understood, who told
Us on our last day at Carstens never to come back
To see her, knowing we never would — she is gone.

But as I walked a second floor hall, smelling wet
Raincoats and dry chalkdust, glancing at the spot
Where Jim Brooks fainted and the doorway where Miss Jollif
Cried, I looked through a door
And saw Miss Adams; she stood beside her desk speaking
To her class with all the spare, graceful aplomb
That must have made some mark on us; she turned, saw me,
Murmured to her class, and came out to the hall.
I am no longer seven or eight or nine — yet she
Gazed at me for a long moment,
Then smiled and said:
"Why, Gerald."

58.

Father Smith. God rewards the very good eternally,
because his goodness is infinite, or without limit. Isn't that
true?
Mr. Jackson. Yes, Father.
Father S. Then He should punish the very wicked eternally,
because His justice is infinite, or without limit. All His
attributes must be equally infinite. God cannot be any more

indifferent toward evil than toward virtue.

Mr. J. That seems very logical.

FATHER SMITH INSTRUCTS JACKSON

I am down in the basement, reading.
The trunks are open and I am looking through the few things
    of mine
That remain in this house. There are four Air Force shirts,
All my report cards, a folder of drawings, some books.
Father Smith evidently has been
Tucked away since my high school
Catechism years, when a group of us met with Father Rispoli
On Monday nights in the rectory. I remember
That Father Smith and Jackson sounded like a couple of
    priests.
I always wished that Jackson had shown more spirit; a touch
Of rebellion would have done wonders.
For instance:

Father S. God rewards the very good eternally, because His goodness is infinite, or without limit. Likewise, He punishes the very wicked eternally, because His justice is infinite, or without limit.

Mr. J. You're guessing.

Father S. Pay attention, Jackson. And show a little respect.

Mr. J. I am. If His goodness is infinite, I've got nothing to worry about.

Father S. Oh yes you do. You could go to hell.

Mr. J. But you said God is just, and that would be very unjust. First I get born, whether I would have wanted to or not. Then suppose I get lousy genes. I have no damn control over anything. I turn out to be weak, bad-tempered, greedy, stupid and lustful. Then I die and I'm supposed to burn in hell for all eternity. If you think that's fair you're full of bananas.

Father S. Try to keep it down, Jackson. Remember, if the sinner be lost, it is wholly his own fault. A person who dies

in the state of sin puts himself in an everlasting state of
refusing God's mercy. God has done more than His part to
save the sinner.

    Mr. J. It sounds to me like somebody's playing favorites.

    Father S. Just as the criminal puts himself in the
penitentiary by his crime, so the lost put themselves in Hell
by their sins.

    Mr. J. Hey, do you want to go bowling?

I placed *Father Smith Instructs Jackson* in a box with
The report cards and shirts. In a moment I will take
    everything out
To a red Mustang I rented this morning.
I've decided to drive back east through Ontario, maybe stop off
In Conestogo for a short look around.
There doesn't seem to be anything
Much else in the trunk — just
A couple of old blankets; a box of our family's best Christmas
Ornaments; an envelope of newspaper clippings
I wish I had time to
Look at; a fox fur piece I remember;
A small box of old letters
Addressed to Miss F. Holm, 822 Windsor Sq.,
Philadelphia, Pa.,
From an R. Prees; and some envelopes with locks of hair
Belonging once to my sister, my brother, and me.
My father has given me a carved table that Opa made
And he said to take along anything else I would like.
I am taking four of the albums with an eye to
Having some copies made.
What if someone had once said to Opa:
"That picture you are about
To take will travel two hundred miles in four
Hours beneath the trunk lid
Of a red Mustang, seventy years from now."
Right now I wish that Father Smith would say

Something very wild
And very true about the future. Of course,
There is the possibility that he already did.

59.

A short time ago we stood on the porch
In November's chill and tried to find last words
That would not be too unusual or somber or too
Blithe. We shook hands and our stubbled cheeks
Touched and I said again the things
Everyone had told him and he said that he would
Do his best. Then we stood for a moment more,
Watching three men unload a van. We saw
A couch go through a door — it was five houses
Up and on the other side, where the Ludwigs lived —
And my father's face was watchful but withdrawn,
The way some old man's may have been, keeping an eye
On us coming in here twenty-eight years before.

I backed the car out. The two of them used to stand there
As I left for east or west, lingering until I was well down
The street, at least till I was past the Pavlicks'.
Perhaps he realized how lonely he looked or perhaps not,
But now with a last smile and wave he went inside
And shut the door.
It must have hit him right away, starting to live alone
For the first time in his life. He must have felt
Cold and tired; I think perhaps he sat down in
The living room and listened to the rooms and let himself
Drift. Perhaps he sat and wondered for a long time
What he should do next.

60.

On my way out of the city
I will stop by Aunt Jo's on Bringard Avenue

Where she lives alone now and see how things go
With her, and talk about the mother and sister
We lately had. I won't stop by the grave,
Not for a while, not until next year.
I've stood at so many in the past: Washington's
And Jefferson's and Mark Twain's beneath the
Tall Elmira elms, Churchill's, even Buffalo Bill's
On his Colorado hill. At these places and at all the others
I would stare at the grass or slab until I had formed
A tender connection, brought them back to life a little,
Saw them sitting, smiling, faintly chatting . . .

Death is the second most important thing that happens
To a life, and pondering one leads inexorably to thoughts of
The other. Grave-tending brings one much or little,
Depending on certain things. For now I'll pass by
My mother's ground and drive and think about her and maybe
Ask her sister about her and be closer to her
Than I would be if I were to position
Myself in section Q of the newly dead,
And wonder, as I sometimes do,
If I'm standing at the feet or at the head.

61.

I carried two albums up the steps
To the door where Aunt Jo waited, smiling,
Wearing a Sunday dress. I was late
And she had begun to think that I'd forgot.
We had tea and biscuits at the kitchen table
While page by page we sifted through
Three quarters of a century.

Two hours later we said good-bye, she with
A quiet sad smile, and I with a stiff new kiss.
Then I went over to Highway 94 and headed

North toward Port Huron and the Bluewater Bridge
To Canada.

I don't remember everything she said or didn't say,
But some of it I do; some will stay,
And I know, because I know Aunt Jo,
That all of it is true; like her sister, she has
Always believed in the blunt fact, come what may.
Now and then she may hold back, but when she
Says a thing at last, when she looks at pages
From the past, watching her you know
That what she says is so.

62.

Eons behind me, eons in front,
Eons above and below, and yet
Momentarily
Here I am,
Dazzled by simple existence,
Awed by land and space and people,
By my sprouting seed and yours;
It is all I need to know to swallow whole
And savor the hours as they roll:
A child's hand to look at or hold; the hot day's
Shower; the winter night's steam; lamplight on
Old wood; wading in a Conestogo stream; the taste
Of tomatoes, good bread, and coffee; the hush after
Bells from a country steeple; the serenity of
Orange blossoms; the casual competence of proud
Plumbers, truckers, farmers, and athletes;
The society of dogs; the grace of cats; a January
Wind over a snow-crusted field; the shy smile
Of a beautiful girl; sun-warmed wooden steps on an
April morning; cut lawns; uncut meadows; people getting

And missing the point — all life's hot and cold and
Medium pleasures and stately foolishments and muddled
Treasures — the little thrill of thoughtful letters,
Rude reminders, won games, heroic actions, unexpected
Replies, endurance, dignity, beginnings of fights,
Impossible feats, the music of masters, walls of books,
Wise old faces, wit and words of love.

Trapped in tedium I sit still
And go back in memory and forward in hope;
I mumble, invent, dream, admit what wisps
And shards show up, store them, guard them,
Freeze and harden them for later need.
For when the king of pain and bad times comes
And comes again, shall I curse conception and
The roaring hours ending, or shall I remember
All those fine running rivulets of lovely life that
Covered and washed me and let me see that use was made
Of this gauzy jot of time?

I hope she had more agreeable moments than
I can ever know. I hope that that is so.
But she did live; she had a life, she had her chance.

As for us, the soon to be dead,
I believe in flourishing.
Nonexistence, if there be such a thing,
Is nothing if not tepid.

63.

The morning air is sharp, and the sun blinds me.
I am curving toward the Bridge to Sarnia;
The lake below looks clear as ever but the paper says no.
I have just left a diner in Port Huron where I had three

Fried eggs and bacon, and I was sitting at the counter
Over a second coffee when a young man, twenty, twenty-one,
Eased down on the stool next to me.
He wore a blue T-shirt and brown corduroy pants.
"Jimmy?" he said to the counterman, "order of toast
With that coffee." His hair, clipped almost to a gray
   nonexistence,
Did little to enhance his round and friendly face.
He turned to me.
"Hey, how you been?"
I looked at him — blankly, I suppose.
"I know you from somewhere. I seen you before."
I shook my head no.
"You not from here? I seen you."
"I've been through here before."
"I must have seen you when you went through."
He moved the sugar closer to himself.
"You never worked here? Welfare office? I know you.
You're not a draftsman? I'm a draftsman by trade."
He leaned back as he saw his coffee coming.
"Thanks, Jimmy. I'm afraid to work any one place. They get
You tied down, you never get away. I keep moving.
Nuts to work. Fish. Hunt. You like to hunt? My buddy shot
   a moose."
"Wouldn't it get boring, not working?"
"They got computers now. Computers do
All the work. You got
A problem, a computer will fix it." He sipped his coffee.
"They got a computer working on my problems."
He stared thoughtfully at the pie shelves, and chewed slowly.
"How many computers do you think there are? In the
   world?"
"I don't know."
"I say a hundred thousand. At least."
Jimmy slid another cup in front of me. The look in his eyes

Was deep and kind.
"Jimmy, him and me,
We're discussing computers, Jimmy. How many
Do you think there are? I say about . . . fifty thousand."
Jimmy looked past us at the street.
Without answering, he walked away
To the other end of the counter.
"They won't need us. What are they going to need us for?"
He began to tap his fingers on the counter. He started to say
Something, then stopped. Finally he said: "The best is
Yet to be. Come grow old along with me, the best is yet to
  be."
He looked at me and smiled. "Browning."
"Was it Robert, or Elizabeth Barrett?" said a woman
Who had just
Sat down on the other side.
"Who's she?"
"They were married and they wrote poetry to each other."
"No kidding? He married a poet? A poet married to a poet?
They didn't tell me about her. I bet she was good."
He turned to me worriedly.
"I only know the guy Browning. They never told me about
  her."

At the cash register Jimmy said quietly: "They had him up
To Newtown. Twice."
"Oh, I see."
"He's okay, though. He hangs around.
He's lonely, you know?
He likes to talk. There's a lot of lonely people around."

As I got into the car, there was a sound at the door of the
  diner.
He was standing there, an anxious look in his eye.
"I wanted to say good-bye!

Take it easy, okay?"
We waved to each other.
I saw him get smaller and smaller in the mirror,
Standing there under the diner's sign.

64.

In Canada, driving east on 7.
My route will take me near London, then on 4 to Elginfield,
Through St. Mary's to Stratford then on 7 and 8 through
Shakespeare and New Hamburg to Kitchener.
Once or twice when
I was young we tried the southern route, taking the tunnel
To Windsor and heading north on
Highway 2, but no one liked
It much; the land was flat, the farms and fields dull and
Not as healthy as they seem to be up here.

Ontario in the 1930s was a child's picture book of the world.
There was a slow honesty to farm, town, road, even directions
At country intersections, each name lettered on its slat
And mounted on the tall post, like a big white coatrack.
There was no barrier between the land and you.
It is still like that
In places, advertising feeble against land and sky; but
Highways are wider now,
And no one touches bushes as he goes by.

Near St. Mary's.
Fields slope off and rise away, curve, stop abruptly against
Pockets of trees. Long straight lanes to brick
Farmhouses. Great silvery gray and airy boarded barns. Steep
And stony ramps. Silverwood Ice Cream. Player's. Sweet
    Caporal.

Not many animals out today; some pigs, a few cows, a horse
or two.

We had three flats one year on a 1932 Dodge, and rolled on
a rim
From Prospect Hill down into St. Mary's. Twelve hours that
year to go 196 miles.
The suitcases were on the running board and the summer heat
Made the mohair upholstery smell. We passed sandwiches
around
And drank lemonade and occasionally shouted to each other
Above the pounding air.
We averaged thirty-five miles an hour
When things went well.

An intersection outside Stratford.
I am parked under a sign that says Wellesley is up this
Road to the north. North Easthope is up there too
Somewhere. My mother always looked in its direction as
We went by. On Saturdays they came down this road
In their horse and buggy and it would take them all day to
Come in and go back. Odd to think that I have pictures and
Furniture with me now that used to be in a house that
Lies up this quiet road. Odd to think
That I have never seen these places.

65.

9 P.M. The Riviera Motor Hotel, Kitchener, Ontario.
North Easthope is not a town, not a village;
It is an area of German farms.
Two long straight gravel roads intersect, and there,
Diagonally across from each other, are the church
And parsonage. I stood in front with the caretaker;
We compared the buildings with the snapshots . . .

In seventy years almost nothing had changed. I took
New pictures from the same spots and saw only that
The trees were taller, the grass shorter, and the
Cemetery fuller. I sat at the organ my mother had
played at sixteen. I pressed the keys and nothing happened.

At the fourth farm from the corner I met Lloyd Schmidt.
He was in my mother's confirmation class; he remembered
That Opa played the violin for them sometimes.
A week ago Schmidt and his wife celebrated
Their fiftieth wedding anniversary. After a while we went
Out to the barn and he showed me through and we stood
Between the pigs and cows and talked.
Then there was a long silence and then he said,
"So she's gone."
The animals had settled down now, with the only sound
An occasional snuffle and the creak of a board.
"She was a pretty thing, you know.
Everybody wanted her."
He looked at me and said, "Reverend Holm,
One time he said to her, 'There is the house
That you will live in.' He meant this house.
He wanted her to marry me."
A fine moist breeze came to us from somewhere.
"But then he was thrown by that horse. And then
They moved to Wellesley. She never did come back here."

We went outside and walked to the car.
A wind came up and it began to rain.
Schmidt laughed shortly and looked at his fields.
"Now that summer's over the skies
Are full of it." We shook hands.
"The last time I saw her was at your grandmother's
Funeral. I went up to her and I said,
'Do you know me?' And she said,
'I could never forget those eyes.'"

66.

I went to Wellesley later in the day,
It wasn't far; the fields were muted tans,
And here a fleck of green; the barns and sky
Were grays, the empty highway white,
My bright-red rented hood dividing all,
Looking good against the grain, the way a tall light-
Painted house looks in a clearing,
Notwithstanding Frank Lloyd Wright.

I wanted to see the house that Opa moved his family
To in 1912, after the accident that shortened
His leg, his stride, and his pastoral career, the house
My mother and Jo left to go to Philadelphia,
The last place they were a family and close.

I sat in the car by the lake in the center of town
And again studied the album, the careful views of kitchen,
Study, coffee on the grass, Friedchen sitting on her
Steamer trunk by the gate, wearing an enormous flowered hat
And toe-length coat and grim expression.
There were Opa and young Rim gazing sternly in fur hats
Out over the lake, and there were all of them canoeing,
An arrow pointing to the house beyond; and so I drove
Around the lake and found the road and drew up to
The house. Such a lovely little shock it was to see it
All the same, door handles, windows, porch supports,
Nothing changed except now higher, wider leafy things . . .
To feel the steps and porch was like walking on old paper —
If it were possible to trespass on time, I was doing it.

The old Mennonite woman who now lives there was wearing
Small round spectacles, a large apron with blue embroidery
At the edges, and what turned out to be a perpetual smile.
At five o'clock on a Saturday evening she had been reading

The family Bible at the kitchen table. She remembered
My mother, invited me in, and took gentle interest in
The album. We wandered from room to room, comparing,
Then sat in the kitchen and talked.
Her older brother, who had lived with her, was in the
    hospital.
Opa had preached once or twice, she knew, at the Lutheran
    Church across
The lake; there, you can just see the steeple above
The trees. She had never heard him.
An old clock ticked slowly, the slowest I ever heard.
She had arthritis. Her hands were stiff and gnarled.
She spoke softly, said sad things, and smiled . . .
Outside I pumped two cups of water at the well
And looked at the barn. My mother had fought in the kitchen
One day with Jo and Rim, tried unsuccessfully to hit them
With a dishcloth while they laughed at her;
Then she hid herself
Away in the barn for hours while the family searched.

"I must warn you," said Oma, "you are getting a spitfire."
"I know, I know," young Floyd replied.

The bells from the church across the lake began to ring.
We walked around to the front and shook hands and
I got in the car and drove away toward Kitchener
And Waterloo. I went slowly by the church.
The bells had rung long and stopped just as I passed.
The vibrations lasted a while longer.

Darkness had fallen over the fields and I was alone
On the highway once more.
CBC brought me news from Windsor,
And a French station in Montreal had movie times.
Behind me an old woman of Wellesley had undoubtedly

Returned to her Bible, and I wondered if there were
Many more across the land doing the same as she.
Probably not. But one doesn't know —
Her kind receive very little publicity.

67.

I was in the town of Flensburg once, on
The Danish border. I wandered through its narrow
Streets and up and down its steps, sketched its shops
And corners and crooked houses, and sat by the water.
Then I bought bread and sausage and walked out of town
And went along the cobbled country road
That led to Copenhagen.

In Detroit a few years later my mother gave me
A four-by-five-inch handmade book. It had a red leather
Binding and gold edging. Its front and back covers were made
Of tiny beads — gold and silver beads and three kinds of blue.
One of Opa's sisters had made it for him and presented it
To him on Christmas eve.
The pages were blank and Opa filled
Them with verses about a girl named Marie, whom he called,
In the German way, Mariechen.

The first is dated the 27th of December, 1879, and was
Written at home in Hütten.
The three last ones are dated 1882,
Kiel. All the others were done in Flensburg.

On the bed beside me now is Opa's
Other book of poetry, given
To me by Aunt Jo. This one is bound
Completely in red leather
And is much larger, 172 pages in heavy stock. It is in good

Condition, with neither smudge nor rip.
The first entry is again
The 27th of December, 1879, but the
Last is in 1918. The handwriting
Becomes larger as years pass, and the color of the ink changes
From light brown to black.
Until page 89, the pieces are either to or about Mariechen.
But under the last stanza there he wrote large and with
Underlined force: FINIS. The date was 22 November, 1883.
Not long after he is in New York. His mother, having borne
Twenty-one children, is dead at forty-eight.
He will not see his father again.

The handwriting is lovely and illegible — the letters formed in
Germanic oldstyle — and translation is difficult. Aunt Jo read
Some of it to me, and it gets easier as you go along. Still,
There is only the bare sense of lines, nothing more. Aunt Jo
Paused once and said, "Maybe that doesn't sound like much,
But in German it's quite beautiful."

So I lie here reading about meetings and departures, of his
Joy and pain, of enforced absences; there was a run to a
    steamship,
A hand pressed in his . . .

> "But we had to say good-bye again,
> Whether for good, God may decide.
> We both had tears in our eyes;
> Alas, for only one year, my heart, you have loved
>   her . . ."

> "Man lives his time, happy to be alive,
> And he enjoys the fruit of his labor.
> Suddenly death comes and they put him
> In the cool grave, deep into the lap of

The good earth and the musty air of the grave.
I cannot escape death that threatens me,
But I would depart unwillingly,
Leaving all that I enjoy.
At my grave the maiden I loved would stand
And weep; I could not see her anymore.
And from the firmament the pale moon
Would shine, as always."

"Your picture, I cannot penetrate the mystery;
I keep studying it, I see no falsehood anywhere.
Isn't it you who wrote the words
That wounded me so deeply?
How can you sadden a faithful heart
With falsehood and deceit?
Haven't you often forgiven me with a loving pressing
Of your hands when we wanted to drink the sweet
Nectar, sip by sip? Didn't I find in your eyes
My peace and quiet when I saw you smile?
Could I not read on your forehead, Faithful until death?
Break your silence and release me from this yoke;
Say you will belong to me again, say
You still are mine!
You press your lips even harder together?
Is it true your love was never real?
The waves ebb away. Only foam remains.
Your picture, I cannot penetrate the mystery;
I keep studying it, I see no falsehood, anywhere."

Eighty-nine years after the date of the first entry,
Following, laboriously, the twists of my grandfather's heart,
I lie propped against pillows, the blinds drawn against the
    neon,
Eight miles from where his dreamer's bones
Are buried in that cool

Grave he spoke of. Born on an island, he became an island.
Lying alone here, no island, a peninsula perhaps, reading
My pre-history, it seems to me it all is good to know.
Did he want the story passed? If not, I think, these volumes
Would have vanished long ago.

68.

I saw three deaf mutes in a restaurant this morning.
One, white-haired, already sat at the counter
When the other two came in and chose places, leaving
Vacant stools between all three.
They ordered coffee with fingers and fists and wide grins
And they thumped the counter and kidded the old one
With low grunts and stabbing gestures.
He angrily waved them off and from then on kept
His eyes on his all-absorbing cereal and cellophaned crackers.
Their speaking fists flashed now and then in his direction
But he never looked up again.
They gave up on him, only looking over smiling
As he sat with cradling arms about his cup and bowl and
    plate.
There are times when even a man who learns to speak late
Has no desire to communicate.

69.

Conestogo.
An unusually warm November morning.
The sky is half filled with pillow-sized
Clouds; sudden floods of sun and shade and sun
Force one's attention again and then again
Upon surfaces of things.

Our end of the village remains, outwardly,
Stuck in time, no new construction, gardens, barns,

Fields and houses unchanged except for one;
But the laying bare and chopping there troubles
Even those without long and hungry ties.
Young Mrs. Knauff said: "It's terrible what he did
To your grandfather's house. We would have bought it
Ourselves only we hadn't the money."
When Oma died Uncle Rim had stayed behind and sold
The house and some of the furniture for thirty-nine
Hundred dollars to a red-headed trucker whose wife
And children soon left him,
Left him living there alone.

The fence is gone, and the barn, the enormous willow
That sheltered it, and every flower and bush and tree
Except three lindens along the side. The well has been
Filled in and the summer kitchen torn off.
Four trucks stand high where the grapevines grew.
Engine parts lie here and there about the yard and two
Charcoal tires ring the spot where the wren's
Birdhouse with its minute hole had perched high
Atop its weathered and wavy pole.
The front and back covers of a copy of *True,*
Once wet, now crisp, crackle beneath the
Chipped legs of a folding chair.
All about me lies evidence of human achievement.
But civilization has fled.

He saw me standing there and came outside
And said that he had known Opa and he remembered
My family and he remembered me as a boy.
I ventured a question: Why were all the trees gone?
He said: "Them three big ones in front, roots were
Working into the cellar."
Inside, a refrigerator stood where the stove had been
And in the darkened dining room a television screen

Flickered in the corner where the china cabinet once was.
He said he was proud of the bathroom he had installed
Where Opa's study had been. The music room was packed
Tight with boxes, tables and chairs, machine parts,
And in a far corner, Opa's desk. On its top lay
A wrench and a couple of rags.
The place had had no plumbing,
He said, poor wiring too, and no insulation in
The walls. He said he'd had a proper time getting it
All in shape. But he felt he was making progress now.
It takes time, he said, to get things done.

The Trail's End Hotel has burned down. The Schweitzers'
Barn has disappeared, and their house, its red bricks
Painted white, is now a home for retarded children.
If it had been my decision to make, I might have
Left them that barn, filled with hay, to play in.
Across the road the doors of the blacksmith shop
Are shut; Mr. Geise, after fifty years of hunching
And pounding and shoving, died of a weakened heart.

The rest of Conestogo looks much as it always did,
Especially here by the cemetery, where change is
Slow, quiet, and unobtrusive.
I strolled about it again as in other years
Because it is both peaceful and peculiarly cheerful
And because I can see the land for miles
And because there are interesting things to read.
Here around me are Oma and Opa, Marty and Charley,
Mr. Kienzle and old George Dahmer, Mrs. Holle,
And Oscar Stroh. And all the other old ones
Who would squint down at me under the July sun
And ask me how I was.
Strange that I know more about these dead ones than
I do the living;

Odd how one is increasingly more admiring of them,
And certainly more forgiving.

70.

I've left Conestogo now; a moment ago I
Drove past Stroh's store, and I thought about
Old Oscar, who died about the time
That Marty Schweitzer did.

Oscar's nephews, Russell and Lester, run the store now;
They've brought it up to date, installed comic book racks
And plastic displays and long fluorescent lights.

But I've been thinking of it as it was
When Oscar was there, nesting behind the worn oak counter
Like a crippled-wing bird, with all his old things
Around, and with his bald head and big mustache and
Brown armbands and crackly voice and his grin; I've
Been remembering how kind he seemed but also how he
Always took my big penny when I ran in there for candy
On cool and sunny mornings, when I wore the scratchy
    sweater
For the chill and the short pants for the noon heat.

Oscar Stroh always looked down fondly at me, saying:
"And how is Opa and Oma?" and I would say "Fine," thinking
That he must know better than I.
And though we were friends, he always took my penny.
I expected it; I understood our bit of commerce.
But yet as I walked out and under the fluttering oaks at
The Trail's End Hotel, rolling the butterscotch in my mouth,
I would be the least bit shocked
That a grown man should be interested in my Canadian
    penny.

71.

I do wonder sometimes
What spiritual or material benefits
My United States has sent north that would make
This Canada land want to rise and bless us . . .
American character and strength has brought down
Tyrants and its hard-earned wealth has gone out
To every kind of victim in every kind of place;
But between disasters, what's our general flow?
The best of our country does not travel well,
While the worst runs wild and scores, partly, perhaps,
Because there's so much more.

Once-virginal villages are not so innocent now;
Describe them as you will, they were at least themselves,
Unknown, uninfluenced, untouched by far-off beasts
With nearby paws.

Once I saw Conestogo people gather close together
At the schoolground after supper to watch their sons
And fathers show off their softball skills, and all
That light humor and easy affection was a
Touching thing to see. Later I saw them in Stroh's,
Yelping over Orange Crush and Cokes, and later still
You could hear them murmuring and laughing softly
On thick-railinged warm night porches.

Now, struck low by TV blight that has blown north
With Dutch elm disease, they hunch alone in half-lit rooms
Under dying trees and study how to imitate
Our finest video minds.

And so I drive along, looking for signs
Of the promising past.

Uniformed guards at border crossings might
Check the papers of people, but no barrier impedes
The flight of beetles, the growth of greed, air and earth and
Mind pollution, the fake and phony and petty, all the
Rolling lonely restless spread of deadening different
Kinds of blight.

72.

Out of Canada, out of Ontario, out of
Waterloo County and Conestogo, out of
The country of memory, I am over the bridge
And east of Buffalo on this cheerless New York
Thruway, these flat fields unknown to me
And unremarkable, as though the land is at rest
After its excessive performance
At the falls.
Later, on 81 south of Syracuse
The sun will light the distant ranges
And toy towns will parade below along the river's notch
And valley farms will fade the dreams and all
I'll have to do is watch.

Near here is Williamsville,
Where Oma and Opa lived their first
Six years together; it's where
My mother was born, where the next child,
Margaret, was born and buried, and where Aunt Jo
Became ill, swollen, fevered, and almost died.
Opa, with one dead daughter a victim of faulty
Diagnosis, determined not to have another; what he
Wanted was another doctor, and he walked eight miles
To reach one.
"They said he saved my life with that eight-mile walk,"

Aunt Jo had told me as we turned the pages. "But your
Mother, she was the one he favored, we all knew that.

"Here she is in this one, sitting on his lap.
That's what I remember.
Oh, they had their troubles too.
They were both so strong-willed, you know.
He'd want his study kept just so,
The curtains and all, and she'd come in and change
Things clear around. Then Opa would come home
And change it back. Would there ever be a fuss!
Oh, she was a crackerjack. Uncle Rim
Could tell you.
She and Opa, they were a pair.
Well, I guess she got it all from him.

"It was the same in Philadelphia.
We lived at 822 Windsor Square, and one day
If she didn't go out and buy a chair and lamp
And a red rug without me knowing a thing about it!
And then she said, come on, you pay for half.
Oh, she was the limit sometimes.
But we had laughs too. She could be fun when
She felt like it. They called her 'Sunny' there
For a while, the staff did. But that name didn't stick.
She had that bad year then.
Oh, that was an awful time.

"I don't know if you ever heard about it;
Well, there's nothing wrong with telling you now.
What happened was, she fell in love.
Here she had turned down I don't know how many,
And at last she fell in love herself.
Doctor Prees, his name was.
I didn't like him much, he was so stern, so stuck-up,

And older, quite a lot older. But she didn't care,
She was just crazy about Doctor Prees.
He was a little like Opa, you see;
That was probably part of it.

"Well, I don't know what finally happened,
But something did. Suddenly it was over.
And oh, did she get low. For almost a year
We had to watch her — we thought — well, you know —
That she might take her life.
We had to keep pills away from her and all that,
Oh, yes, and she was sick in bed for quite a spell.
I was beginning to think she never would
Come out of it. She did though, finally,
But my, we were so scared.

"I don't know what ever became of Doctor Prees.
We left and came here to Detroit, and then of course
She met your dad, and I always liked Floyd.
He was always smiling, easy to get along with,
And he'd just go along with her. I don't know
If I've ever really seen Floyd get mad.
Now if she had married someone like Doctor Prees,
Both of them so headstrong,
Well, I don't see how it would have worked.
I could be wrong, but that's the way I see it.
I don't know what your mother would
Have said. We never spoke about it.
She probably would have refused to.

"Well it's over now.
What's past is past.
As Opa used to say,
'So be it.'"

73.

I am almost home now.
The highway is wet and the sky is growing dark.

Back there when it was time to go,
My father sat in a chair downstairs
While I packed my bag on the trunk at the foot of her bed.
I set my bag in the hall, then washed my hands
In the bathroom. I stood there with my eyes closed,
Thinking about how it looks at two in the night:
Old, cold, dimly white, the nightlight making
Distorted shadows. What a last thing to see.

For twenty-eight years, ill, uneasy, she had been rising aching
In the night to get a drink, take a pill, stare down
At the dark yard, and on unbearable summer nights
Splash water on her face and arms.
What a familiar, dreary sight, that night scene.
The last time she must have awakened, seen that
The clock said only two, and sat on the edge of the bed
For a moment, thinking perhaps of sleepless hours ahead.
Then she rose stiffly, her back or head or arthritic hands
Hurting, and, steadying herself in the doorway, went
Into the hall. Behind her on the dresser the electric fan
Droned on, as it did winter and summer, lulling her
And sheltering her from outside sounds.
Ahead was the faint light, and twenty-eight years of intimate
    shapes;
Then she was at the bathroom door, her eyes on the
Low marble slab — she had stumbled so often lately —
Then she took a step, her very last, and either
She thought, "I wonder if this is it," or else
Consciousness fled instantly and left her
Unseeing and helpless, sinking to the stone floor.

Along one wall there is an old Singer sewing machine;
Her head must have lain near it,
Near the iron pedal and heavy wheel that I
Unwillingly dusted when I was small and called her Mama.
I wish I could have been there.
I wish she could have looked at me for a moment
And I could have cradled her head in my arms and
Touched her face with my hand and told her without feeling
Frozen and false that I loved her, that she had always
Been loved more than she thought.
For there was a bond between us. I did partly understand
Her. I had grown inside her body. A true mother
Ought not to die without seeing a tear on the face
Of a child who loved her in a way he does not
Understand just as he does not understand the rest of it.

When had I last called her Mama?
I wonder when the very last time was.
Maybe it was when I was nine, maybe thirteen.
The final time you call your mother Mama
Is a sweet and shady moment that isn't noticed,
But privately somehow should be marked down.

I left the bathroom and picked up my bag in the hall.
I would not see these rooms again.
My father would move.
I turned off the light, and I stood there.
I looked at the wallpaper.
Somewhere inside me, somebody's small voice said:
"Good-bye, Mama."

ટ૭ ટ૭

At the end of her life days were as long
And baffling as when she was a child in the summer grass.

She lay in a faded housedress on the sofa and waited,
And waited,
And listened to the traffic.
She dozed and woke and dozed and thought:
How was my life so short with days like these?
Her life: it was an afternoon in Waterloo Park,
But not that happy.

It had its moments, though.